Hypertension
and Nutrition

Also by Eric R. Braverman, M.D.

The Healing Nutrients Within:
Facts, Findings and New Research
on Amino Acids
(with Carl C. Pfeiffer, M.D., Ph.D.)

Hypertension and Nutrition

Eric R. Braverman, M.D.

with Matthew Taub, M.D.

Keats Publishing, Inc. New Canaan, Connecticut

Hypertension and Nutrition is intended solely for informational and educational purposes, and not as medical advice. Please consult a medical or health professional if you have questions about your health.

HYPERTENSION AND NUTRITION

Library of Congress Cataloging-in-Publication Data

Braveman, Eric R.
  Hypertension and nutrition / by Eric R. Braverman.
     p.   cm.
  Includes bibliographical references and index.
  ISBN 0-87983-688-1
  1. Hypertension—Diet therapy.   2. Vitamins—Therapeutic use.
  3. Dietary supplements.   I. Title.
RC685.H8B3956   1995
616.1'320654—dc20   95-49091
                                                                    CIP

Printed in the United States of America

Keats Publishing, Inc.
27 Pine Street (Box 876)
New Canaan, Connecticut 06840-0876

98 97 96   6 5 4 3 2 1

Acknowledgments

Thanks are due the following persons:

Joel Fuhrman, M.D., for the strict vegetarian diet;

Francis Goulart for assistance in preparing segments of the material;

Susan Laird, M.A., for proofreading;

Matthew Taub, M.D., for assistance in preparing segments of this material;

E. Weisberg, M.D., for assistance in preparing segments of this material;

The Journal of Orthomolecular Medicine, for permission to use Eric R. Braverman, M.D. and E. Weissberg, B.A., Nutritional Treatments for Hypertension, 7:4, 1992.

Contents

Contents

A Comment from
nutrition authority Gary Null, Ph.D.

"Finally a book that says it all and says it with such common sense easily understood principles that it will serve as the ultimate reference in the field. Another outstanding book by one of America's leading educators in health and nutrition."

Preface

I am offering in this book a very simple five-point program to lower blood pressure, cholesterol, and reduce weight without drugs. The basic parts of the program are:

- Low-carbohydrate, high-protein diet with polyunsaturated oil.
- Dr. Braverman's Hypertension (high blood pressure) multivitamin.*
- Supplementation with fish oil and other nutrients in some cases.
- Supplementation with primrose oil or a polyunsaturated oil.
- Cranial Electrical Stimulation (CES), biofeedback, and total relaxation techniques.

These basic points will lower the blood pressure and reduce the weight of most mild and moderate hypertensive patients. Hundreds of scientific articles can document this program. This can improve the quality of lives of as many as 30 to 50 million Americans who now need one or more daily drug treatments.

The very same program that reverses hypertension also reverses heart disease. Hypertension is frequently just the first step on the way to hardening the whole heart and cardiovascular system. The key to this program is that it lowers cholesterol to 100-150 in virtually all cases, and sometimes cholesterol is lowered to 70. This leads to reversal of heart disease and arteriosclerosis wherever it is in the body—from

---

*These can be prepared at home or, if preferred, ordered by mail. Ingredients appear in the Appendix.

the brain to the legs to the heart. If nutrition does not do it, chelation may do it, or biofeedback, or CES, or drugs. And so it is a complete program.

Another reason why you should use this program is: the *Journal of the American Medical Association,* vol. 272(1994), shows that drug combinations interact and lead to problems for persons with high blood pressure.

Hypertension and Nutrition

Chapter 1

Beyond the Hypertension Hype: Why Drugs Are Not the Answer

"Can there be worse sickness," asked the poet John Donne in 1612, in *The Anatomy of the World*, "than to know that we are never well, nor can be so?"

Donne could have been talking about hypertension (high blood pressure) and heart disease, the number one health threat of the 1990s—a disorder that makes both patients and most doctors despair and turn to medication. Hardening of the arteries begins in your twenties, and you cannot start this program soon enough.

It's hard to believe that you're dying if you're up and doing—but it's true if you have high blood pressure, the "Silent Killer." That's hypertension's calling card. It's painless, often symptomless, and unlike other cardiovascular disorders, it doesn't give you time to pack your bags. Fifteen to 20 percent of adults in the United States have hypertension. The great majority of cases are presently undetected, untreated or inadequately treated, and it's twice as life-threatening if you don't know you have it. High blood pressure takes years to develop and up to 30 years to do its damage—not just to your heart and arteries, but to your kidneys, lungs, brain and nervous system.

Next to old age and obesity, high blood pressure is the most potent predictor of a shortened life span. Of the 60 million Americans who are hypertensive, 10 million or more

1

may be on medication of questionable value or real documented danger.

Hypertension is the prime contributing factor to coronary heart disease and stroke. If you have hypertension, you are beginning to have heart disease. And if you have an elevated total cholesterol level, elevated serum triglycerides, or a decreased level of good (HDL) cholesterol, you are a candidate for other serious health problems, including diabetes and kidney disease. But the good news about this bad news disorder is that it responds well and rapidly to the *right* treatment. And that treatment is the drug-free no-more-hypertension program which I have used to return over 1,000 patients to a normal life at my Princeton Associates for Total Health (PATH) Center in Princeton, New Jersey. It's the first *safe* do-it-yourself-with-your-doctor program for lowering your blood pressure without drugs for life.

Why Drugs Are Not the First Answer

If you have your heart set on a long, happy, healthy, productive life—in spite of your hypertension—revise your forecast if you are using drugs to reach that goal.

Current reports by the American Medical Association, the American Heart Association, and the National Institutes of Health indicate that treating your high blood pressure (HPB) with the drugs in current use can reduce sex drive, produces accelerated aging of all the major organs—the heart, brain, lungs and kidneys—and can shorten your life by 16 years (or more if you are ten or more pounds overweight—and 85 percent of all hypertensives are). You are among the walking wounded, whether you have conventional treatment with drugs as one out of every five hypertensives do, or go *without* any treatment, as 80 percent of all hypertensives do. Those taking drugs are receiving treatment that masks symptoms and in some cases actually hardens arteries and makes the condition worse. If your cholesterol is not low enough, then you are still hardening, and the drugs that you are taking may be making your condition worse.

Consider **diuretics,** which are often the first line of treatment for hypertension. Did you know that they deplete your body of the healthy heart minerals magnesium and potassium, in addition to damaging the kidneys with long-term use, raising cholesterol levels and increasing your risk of fatal heart irregularities? Or that the incidence of sudden death among long-term diuretics users is high? (When low doses don't do the job, doctors are more likely to increase the dose rather than discontinue the medication.) Or that beta-blockers, also among the first drugs administered in the so-called "stepped care" approach, often lead to long-term depression, reduced sexual function and dependency on unnecessary antidepressants?

See the following tables for additional risk factors.

Those Bitter Pills

THE HAZARDS OF PRESCRIPTION HYPERTENSION DRUGS

There are five classes of drugs used to treat hypertension. You could be taking two, four, or eventually *all* of the killers below. It is not that drugs are all killers but the side effects, without vitamins and nutrients, are dangerous. Here's what you're in for with each—and in the last column what you will be substituting on the Braverman Program *to produce the same benefits without the risk.* (Details on these nutritional substitutions in Chapter 5.)

CLASS 1

Class I	Action	Side Effects	Alternative Nutrients
Thiazide and/ or potassium sparing e.g., Diuril, Lasix, furosemide, Dyazide	Remove sodium and fluids from the body	Sexual dysfunction; depletes body of the heart-health minerals, potassium and magnesium; causes fatigue, muscle spasms; long-term use damages kidneys. Raises cholesterol, lowers HDL, and increases heart arrhythmia and sudden death	Borage oil Safflower oil High-protein diet

CLASS 2

Alpha- and Beta-Blockers	Action	Side Effects	Possible Alternative Nutrients
Beta-blockers propranolol (Inderal), Alpha-blockers Prazosin (Minipress) Diuretic: spironolactone	Blocks (alpha) adrenaline, lowers blood pressure by making heart beat less frequently (beta).	Increased depression and myocardial infarction after prolonged use. Breast enlargement (spiro-nolactone); narrows bronchial tubes; insomnia, sleep disorders; fatigue; constipation, slowed heartbeat, dizziness; fainting (postural hypotension), impotence, headaches; depression	CoQ10 Garlic Taurine Magnesium Potassium

Sympatholytics	Action	Side Effects	Possible Alternative Nutrients
Clonidine (Catapres), Methyldopa (Aldomet), reserpine (Serpasil)	Inhibits sympathetic nervous system; reduces cardiac output	Sedative effect; postural hypotension; sexual dysfunction; disabling depression (reserpine); anemia; hepatitis (clonidine)	

CLASS 3

Vasodilators (often pre-scribed with a diuretic)	Action	Side Effects	Possible Alternative Nutrients
Hydralazine (Apresoline), Minoxidil, Loniten (often used with a beta-blocker)	Open up arteries, relaxes constricted vessels	Alters heart function; increases coronary heart disease risk; fluid retention; increased heartbeat; stimulates hair growth (Minoxidil)	B6 Borage oil Calcium Garlic Magnesium Safflower oil Taurine, etc.

CLASS 4

The Best Group New Drugs	Action	Side Effects	Possible Alternative Nutrients
Angiotensin-2 blockers, Captopril (Capoten), Enalapril (Vasotec)	Inhibits vascular constriction; causes sodium retention	Impaired immune response due to reduced white blood cell count; loss of pro-tein in urine, dry throat, fatigue, etc.	None

Calcium Channel Blockers	Action	Side Effects	Possible Alternative Nutrients
Diltiazem (Cardizem), Nifedipine (Procardia), Verapamil (Calan and Isoptin)	Used to treat angina and high blood pressure in the elderly	Abnormal slowing of heartbeat aggravates congestive heart failure	Magnesium
Last Resort Medications Guanethidine (Ismelin)		Depletes Norepine-phrine at nerve ends; severe sexual dysfunction, etc.	

BUT THAT'S NOT ALL

One drug leads to another. The dose that lowered your blood pressure and treated your heart disease last month may not do the trick this month so your doctor prescribes a bigger dose or an additional drug. It's a vicious circle. Drugs treat the symptoms, which can be necessary, but getting at the root cause requires nutrition, diet and lifestyle changes. Furthermore, all too many individuals are addicted. Here are a few of the sad facts:

■ 50 percent of all elderly patients on Thiazide diuretics show severe potassium or magnesium deficiencies in the blood and skeletal muscle.

■ Aldomet—also known as methyldopa—severely impairs sexual function, mood and overall quality of life, and can cause hemolytic anemia.

■ Diuretics, which are the most commonly prescribed HBP drugs, continue to have the largest variety of side effects. They increase the possibility of severe life-threatening arrhythmias and raise cholesterol, triglycerides, and other dangerous fat factors in the blood. Patients on diuretics have an increased risk of death due to myocardial infarction or sudden death and diuretics can poison and damage the kidneys.

■ After three years of beta-blockers, the heart muscle can significantly weaken. Beta-blockers worsen asthma and increase depression (25 percent of all patients on blockers eventually must be treated with antidepressant drugs). In the long run, they *increase* your risk of a coronary event.

■ Alpha-blockers are not particularly helpful in long-term HBP treatment, causing sedation, constipation, dizziness, and—in the case of methyldopa—lowered work performance and general well-being.

■ Hydralazine removes the healthy immune-system nutrient manganese from your body, boosts blood pressure, and can lead to seizures.

■ Most HBP drugs interfere with normal brain function, decrease alertness and memory, and can cause premature senility symptoms in patients over 60. These side effects are greatly reduced by nutrients.

■ Angiotensin-2 inhibitors may decrease your body reserves of the trace minerals (copper, zinc, selenium) which protect your immune system.

■ Even the *best* of the HBP drugs, the so-called angiotensin-2 blockers (Captopril, Vasotec) worsen the quality of life for 30 to 40 percent of all patients.

■ Up to 50 percent of all patients on methyldopa, captopril, or propranolol experience fatigue and lethargy; up to 30 percent have some form of sexual disorder; over 10 percent have sleep disorders, nightmares, headaches, anxiety, irritability, palpitations, dry mouth, dizziness, nausea, and muscle cramps. Nutrients, biofeedback, exercise and this total reversal program are necessary to reverse developing heart disease now, *early*, **before it is too late.**

■ 30 percent of all hypertensives on alpha-blockers suffer from sexual disorders. Sexual problems are the second most common side effect of hypertension and heart medication. Drugs for hypertension not only kill your sex drive, they kill you. Nutrients, natural testosterone, and herbs like Yocon can rebuild your sex life.

■ This increased mortality is also found in patients treated with the cholesterol-lowering drugs clofibrate and Lopid. Try to use these drugs sparingly. Furthermore, drugs like Provocol and Zocor deplete serotonin and CoQ10, and patients can become more accident-prone.

■ In general, most hypertension drugs cause mental depression and damage the circulatory system in the long run, deplete the body's store of the major minerals potassium and magnesium, and increase cholesterol and triglycerides.

WHAT'S THE ALTERNATIVE?

You can't afford to take the wrong steps or to take no steps at all. Even the slightest elevation in blood pressure cannot be dismissed . . . and studies indicate that blood pressure that yo-yos may be more dangerous than blood pressure that remains consistently high.

Do you want to keep footing the bill for a lifetime of medicine that ironically enough *increases* your risk of heart attack, stroke and early death? Such "help" doesn't come cheap. The cost of controlling hypertension with medication for a lifetime can run into hundreds of thousands of dollars, and even more than that if the cost of treating the side effects produced by such drugs is considered. If you're sick of being sick and are ready to consider a cost-sensible alternative with a near 100-

percent return in terms of health benefits and monetary gain, you're ready for this How to Lower Your Blood Pressure and Reverse Heart Disease Naturally program.

Even if your doctor has categorized you as "high risk," my No-More-Hypertension program, which is completely detailed in the following pages, can return you to a normal life—in only 30 to 90 days.

My program gets results whether you are suffering from mild, borderline, moderate, or even severely high blood pressure. It lowers blood pressure as high as 180/120 to 120/80, cholesterol as high as 400 to 180, and triglycerides as high as 1800 to normal levels—in 30 to 90 days:

■ By replacing dangerous hypertension-lowering drugs with safe hypertension-lowering food supplements that work like drugs—but without the health-damaging side effects.
■ By replacing the key high-risk, heart disease and hypertension-making foods you eat with key no-risk, heart disease and hypertension-breaking foods. Did you know that improper diet accounted for more than two-thirds of the millions of deaths in the U.S. last year? Diet is one of the three major causative factors in hypertension.
■ By helping you to break the bad habits that set you up for heart disease and hypertension in the first place, smoking, overeating, stress, and too much salt, sugar, alcohol, and caffeine. And by starting you on daily stress control and easy exercise plans.

My treatment program, in 95 percent of the cases, is drug-free within a few weeks. If your condition is severe, you may need to continue some medication, usually temporarily. If you continue to work at it, chelation, biofeedback, diet and vitamins need to be applied continually in your life.

My program will work no matter how much it differs from those you've read about in my case histories, owing to the fact that no two hypertension victims are alike—sex, heredity, cholesterol level and age are all variables to consider as you customize the program to meet your needs.

In addition, as a by-product of my program, there are these benefits:

- You will improve the general quality of your life along with restoring your sexual vitality;
- Improve your immunity to cancer;
- Improve your life span;
- And you will lower your body's toxic metal levels through the use of nutrients and chelation, and experience relief from any hidden food allergies you may have. (Allergies, toxic metals, and all forms of stress are blood pressure boosters.)

No *one* factor alone can alter your already adversely altered body chemistry—but the right combination can, and I've arrived at the combination after ten years of treating hypertension and heart disease. If you care enough to follow this simple step-by-step program, you can turn your health around in one month's time and become the hypertension-free, healthy human being you were meant to be with a low cardiovascular risk that will last for life. Your cholesterol will lower, your HDL will change, and you will be on the way to wellness. Remember, this is a lifetime effort with great benefits.

A Day in the Life of a Hypertensive: The Way It Is

They call it the "silent killer." Hypertension is anything *but.* Once you know you've got it, life will never be the same, especially if the doctor has you on a typical regimen which is nutritionally ill-suited to hypertension and heart disease control. Ironically, even the AMA now recommends the dietary approach as the first line of treatment for mild and moderate hypertension.

Depending on your condition and your physician, you may

be taking as few as one or as many as a dozen medications a day. Typical intake is one to three medications.

Drugs are part of the day for many of the nation's 10 million victims of the country's most devastating but least understood threat. Are you included? How familiar does the following scenario sound?

At 7 a.m. it's time to get up and take your first blood pressure reading of the day. It's 150/90, 10 points lower than last night and still in the "mild" range. So far so good. Now for breakfast—first "deprivation" meal of the day. Because salt, fat, cholesterol, and extra calories are all risk factors according to your doctor, breakfast consists of one thin slice of unbuttered whole-wheat toast, scrambled eggs (whites only) seasoned with a salt substitute, fruit juice and a cup of decaffeinated coffee with a fatty, nondairy creamer. To reduce the volume of plasma in your body and remove excess sodium you take a Lozol, your first diuretic of the day, and prepare for one of the several side effects you usually experience.[1]

What will it be today? The overwhelming lethargy that puts you to sleep on your hour's commute to the office? Will you feel washed out all day? The rippling muscle spasms in your legs and feet that sometimes paralyze you—right in the middle of an important meeting with a new client or the boss? Or will it be a further reduction in sexual stamina—ruining something that used to be the high point of your hard-working day?

Next, some mild, doctor-prescribed, midmorning exercise (perhaps a brisk walk to a nearby city park and back). This is to help regulate your heart rhythm. Intense exercise, which boosts blood pressure to 200 systolic and 100 diastolic and accelerates heart rate, can be dangerous. A gradual elevation in blood pressure is more desirable—e.g., walking, slow bicycling, low-impact aerobics.

You get ready for your second meal and second drug of the day. Today it's no-sodium cream of celery soup from a can, with salt-free crackers and a piece of fresh fruit to supply fiber and the minerals you lack when you're hypertensive, according to

your doctor. Plus a salt-free seltzer to down drug number two —
a beta-blocking agent called Inderal. You remind yourself why
you need *this* pill: According to the doctor, it's the only way to
prevent a buildup of excess adrenaline which boosts blood pressure. Yet Inderal often makes you depressed, sometimes nau-
seous or dizzy. Maybe today it only makes you a little groggy.[2]

Finishing your seltzer, you remember that your doctor has
added a second drug to your midday meal—a vasodilator
called Loniten, which serves the purpose of opening up and
relaxing constricted arterioles. And because a vasodilator can
cause rapid and extreme water retention, there's another diuretic to take. It's hard to know what's worse—the water
retention itself or the drug that counteracts it.[3]

Dinner won't exactly make your day either, since you like
to eat. After a no-cocktail hour (alcohol and caffeine—both
blood pressure boosters—are off the menu) you sit down to
a dinner you *might* have enjoyed if you weren't on medication: filet of flounder broiled and served with a no-fat wine
sauce, baked potatoes and steamed green beans—plus a 95 percent fat-free, imitation ice cream. But the prospect of downing
another drug—this time an angiotensin converting enzyme
blocker called Capoten—takes the pleasure out of the meal.
Side effects may stop at a dry mouth if you're lucky, but you've
read the medical literature and this one's a bitter pill to swallow.
According to the *Physician's Desk Reference*, side effects of Capoten and other angiotensin enzyme blockers include possible
kidney failure, loss of protein in the urine, increased risk of
heart attack and a shortened life span. Most common side effects
are fatigue and sexual dysfunction, and these are the least severe. It takes more than a little bit of sugar to make medicine
like this go down, especially if you are not taking your vitamins—which can counteract many of the side effects.

And bedtime isn't the happy prospect it used to be either,
since the last thing you will be enjoying is sex or a good
read—thanks to the pre-lights out medication your doctor just
added to your medication menu. This one, clonidine, lowers

blood pressure by changing the way your sympathetic nervous system works. Unfortunately, you've discovered it also reduces sexual drive and performance, just like Lozol.[4]

Your wife says she understands that your temporary impotence is a side effect of these drugs you need to take—but *does* she? And do you really need all these drugs? You ask yourself this every day. How much damage are they doing to the rest of your body, you wonder. And how long will you be taking them?

A day like the above—which millions of men and women face every day—is better than dying, but not by all that much. There are more pleasurable ways to spend the next 24 hours of your life, even though you have hypertension. My program is proof that every day with hypertension can be worth living. The vitamins, diet, chelation, biofeedback and CES (cranial electrical stimulation, a remarkable technique explored in Chapter 12) will give you a well-being that is better than before you became ill. You will be surprised at how good you can feel. You will learn how to diet the right way with appetizing menus; learn how fish oils, vegetable oils (especially safflower oil and oil of primrose) can replace diuretics and beta-blockers; learn how niacin can replace vasodilators; and learn how nutrients in general can replace drugs. And if you need natural estrogen, progesterone, testosterone, or DHEA, they will revitalize your tired glands and body.

NOTES

1. Diuretics such as Lozol commonly used to treat hypertension produce as many as 25 documented side effects, including irregular heart rhythm, elevation of uric acid (which can lead to gout), nausea and dizziness, in addition to loss of sexual drive, muscle spasms, and lethargy. What is worse is the increased heart disease and hardening of the arteries caused by raising cholesterol levels.
2. This widely used blocking agent and others like it (such as Tenormin) also produce fatigue, insomnia, depression, sex-

ual dysfunction, possible nerve damage, and even increase the risk of coronary heart disease.

3. Vasodilators are sometimes prescribed with *both* a diuretic and a beta-blocker. Other side effects include a rapid pulse, increased risk of stroke and, in the case of Loniten (minoxide), accelerated hair growth (now used as a cream for vertex baldness).

4. The longer it's taken, the worse the effect. Clonidine also puts your brain to sleep and can lead to both anemia and induce hepatitis as an allergic reaction. And does your doctor know that it has proven less effective than it was previously believed to be? In addition, it may shorten your life span by years. If you need drugs, let us start with magnesium; with channel-blockers (Procardia, Cardizem, Kalin) which are probably the best, even more effective when combined with a total health program.

A Day in the Life of a Hypertensive on the Braverman No-More-Hypertension Program

THE NUTRITION PRESCRIPTION: SAY YES TO NUTRIENTS, NO TO DRUGS

The foundation of my nutrient program is fish oil, garlic, primrose oil, magnesium, vitamin B6, taurine, and the other nutrients that appear below. It takes one session to learn how to use the nutrients in the diet, and virtually no case of high blood pressure, high cholesterol, high triglycerides, nor obesity cannot be helped—and usually solved—through proper nutrition, diet and lifestyle changes.

What sets my program apart from all other blood pressure control programs is that it utilizes a number of supplements and foods, not a "miracle vitamin" or single nutritional substance. This results in a restoration of biochemical balance of your whole body—not just the health of your vascular system—because in high blood pressure, the mechanisms can be multiple and can reach many organs. Kidneys, brain and lungs may all be factors. Most of the blood pressure nutrient techniques affect the heart, circulatory system and kidneys. An increased flow to the kidney uses linoleic acid and vitamin B6. To vasodilate thin blood (i.e., reduce platelet stickiness), EPA, garlic, vitamin C, magnesium and niacin are used. To help the heart's pumping action, taurine, calcium, magnesium and potassium are helpful. Other therapies (zinc and molybdenum) increase the excretion of toxic chemicals (lead and cadmium) which can be found in polluted water or cigarettes that can raise blood pressure. Yet most of these nutrients are combined into one pill—the Hypertension Formula (See Appendix.) If these nutrients are not strong enough, then chelation can remove the toxins, while CES and biofeedback may relax your nervous system, along with amino acids to lower your adrenals and lower your blood pressure.

My corrective diet affects primarily the kidneys (low salt), the pancreas (low carbohydrates) or the heart and cardiovascular system. Hence, the diet and nutrition therapy affect the heart, kidneys, pancreas, and peripheral vascular system. Drug modalities which affect the enzymes in the lungs or the brain are likely to have the most additive value. Along with the addition of nutrients, it's important to eliminate caffeine, stimulants, and to lower fat in the diet. The entire program lowers cholesterol and triglycerides as well as blood pressure. When the cholesterol/HDL ratio reaches 2.5, reversal of heart disease occurs. This is the key to understanding how nutrients, fish oil, chelation, and the total wellness program works. Your ratio will change and your own blood scavenger system will clean out your heart for you. The body itself will reverse the disease.

One set of drugs affects the lungs' role in hypertension; specifically, the angiotensin-2 blockers (Captopril, Vasotec), which are compatible with a nutrient program.

Here is what you will be taking daily:

■ 7 Hypertension Multi Formula;

- 7 high-potency capsules of primrose oil, or borage oil, or other source of GLA;
- 7 capsules of high-potency fish oil or 3 tablespoons of liquid EPA emulsified fish oil. There are many other options as well, such as 2 tablespoons of olive oil (30–150 mg);
- CoQ10 (Coenzyme Q10);
- 1 to 2 tablespoons of safflower oil;
- 10 mg of potassium 2 times per day;
- the amino acids arginine and cysteine;
- vitamin C and other vitamins at higher doses;
- and calcium.

(Note: Every supplement program is slightly different and nutrients may be added or subtracted as you progress.)

Chelation is another great way to lower blood pressure since high doses of magnesium lower blood pressure and the chelation process uses high doses of magnesium. EDTA and amino acids that scrape through your bloodstream usually result in the elimination of toxic metals such as lead and cadmium, lower blood pressure gradually, and reverse hardening of the arteries in some cases. With a complete program, we have seen progress in reversing major blockages as part of the entire program. It is doubtful that chelation alone will accomplish this goal, but when combined with all these other techniques, it is a helpful addition. It can certainly help increase collaterals. Chelation as a single-agent therapy needs further documentation. Keep in mind that heavy metals raise cholesterol, and that the program detoxifies the body. EDTA is a natural antioxidant (chelation therapy includes EDTA, magnesium and vitamins).

Chapter 5, "Nutritional Treatments for Hypertension," contains a detailed discussion of the extent, nature and treatment of high blood pressure and the properties and effects of the individual nutrients used in my program.

Your Nutrient Program Treatment of Hypertension: How It Works

OILS

Generic or Trade Name and Dose	Mode of Action and Result	Possible Side Effects at High Dose
Eicosapentaenoic acid (EPA-DHA) and Docosahexaenoic acid 2–15 grams	PGE2 inhibitor vasodilator lowers triglycerides, raises HDL, and antiplatelet	belching bruising
Evening primrose (or borage or black currant) oil (Gamma-linoleic acid) 1–5 grams	PGE 1, 3 promoter diuretic lowers cholesterol	diarrhea
Linoleic acid (safflower, sunflower, linseed oil) 2–20 grams	diuretic lowers cholesterol	diarrhea
Olive oil 2–20 grams	lowers cholesterol raises blood pressure	diarrhea
CoQ10 (Ubiquinone) 30–150 mg	lowers aldosterone lowers angiotensin	diarrhea

PGE = prostaglandins

MINERALS

Generic or Trade Name and Dose	Mode of Action and Result	Possible Side Effects at High Dose
Potassium 10–30 mg	incr. sodium excretion decr. volume	ulcer indigestion heart attack
Magnesium (oxide or hydroxide or sulfate) 1–3 grams	calcium channel vasodilator deficiency state	diarrhea tetany
Zinc (gluconate, chelate) 15–20 mg	Pb, Cd, Al antidote	nausea anemia neutropenia
Calcium (carbonate, citrate) 1–3 grams	increased PGE2 decreased 1, 25 incr. Na excretion	constipation kidney stones
Selenium (selenite) 100–400 mcg	antidote Hg prevents MI	hematuria
GTF (chromium)	prevents MI 200–1000 mcg	flatulence

Al = aluminum; Hg = mercury; Cd = cadmium;
GFT = glucose tolerance factor; MI = myocardial infarction;
Na = sodium; Pb = lead.

AMINO ACIDS
(BUILDING BLOCKS OF PROTEIN)

Generic or Trade Name and Dose	Mode of Action and Result	Possible Side Effects at High Dose
Taurine 1–5 grams	incr. inotrope, decr. cholesterol deficiency	gastritis flatulence
Methionine, Cysteine 1–3 grams, 2–7 grams	Antioxidant, decr. arteriosclerosis	flatulence
Arginine 1–4 grams	decr. cholesterol	arthritis
Tryptophan 3–7 grams	decr. blood pressure	

VITAMINS

Generic or Trade Name and Dose	Mode of Action and Result	Possible Side Effects at High Dose
Niacin (B3) 400 mg–3 grams	vasodilator	flushing itching
Pyridoxine (B6) 200 mg–1 gram	diuretic	neuropathy
Vitamin C 2–7 grams	heavy metal antidote vasodilation	flatulence
Pantetheine	decr. triglycerides	

NUTRIENTS WHICH ARE ALSO USED AS FOODS

Generic or Trade Name and Dose	Mode of Action and Result	Possible Side Effects at High Dose
Garlic 1–2 grams	antioxidant antiplatelet	bad breath indigestion
Fiber—found in grains, fruits, vegetables (varies by plan)	lowers cholesterol regulates bowels	
Pectin	lowers cholesterol	constipation

Chapter 2

The Braverman No-More-Hypertension and Heart Disease Diet Plan

Doing Some Thinking

Think fresh fish, chicken, turkey, vegetable oils, high potassium fruits, vegetables and salad greens, with lots of seasoning, and you're home free. Foods from these groups are the anchor ingredients of my diet in both its forms (except in Plan B with normal weight, eat lots of whole grain).

Eating your fill of these foods daily will automatically give you the nutrients you do need and eliminate the health hazardous foods you don't need to normalize your blood pressure. Here's how and why it works.

If a furnace is loaded with paper, cardboard or wood, what burns first? Obviously, paper, then cardboard, then wood. The same is true when the body ingests carbohydrates, fat and protein. Carbohydrates burn first. Hence, pasta and sugar provide relatively quick energy. Fat burns next; hence, sausage and butter keep a person warm in the winter. Finally, protein burns third; a good steak is slow to give energy but can maintain energy for the longest period.

Therefore, a high-protein diet, when combined with low complex carbohydrates, results in the body eliminating excess

23

water and reversing the hyperinsulinism of hypertension. We can all remember the protein-starved Biafrans, whose bodies swelled up with water. In contrast, a high-protein diet leads to dehydration. This high-protein diet can be dangerous without medical supervision. Dangers with the diet can usually be eliminated by adding fruit, potassium or carbohydrates to the diet. This helps weight loss, heart failure, and especially hypertension. Side effects can be prevented by vitamins. Hence you must take supplements on this diet, especially potassium if fruits are limited for weight concerns. Besides putting a brake on your blood pressure, Diet A is a weight loss plan, but you won't have to count calories. You will lose weight as your system resumes its normal functioning and becomes balanced again as a response to the therapeutic doses of nutrients and the special foods the diet concentrates on.

The diet is also useful for anxiety, hypoglycemia, and depression, because the lack of stimulants and the high amino acid content may lead to steadier nerves and better neurotransmission in the brain. Diet A automatically excludes many common food allergens such as wheat, yeast, peanuts and chocolate and perhaps some unhealthful effects.

The diet has two forms. Follow Plan A if you need to lose weight. After your weight is normalized, switch to Diet B for maintenance. Diet A is a high-protein, moderately low-fat, very low-carbohydrate plan. (Carbohydrates stimulate the appetite and cause the liver to accelerate its production of cholesterol. Carbohydrates actually raise blood pressure in obese individuals.) Diet B allows you more calories and complex carbohydrates, and is appropriate from the start for hypertensives with normal weight.

Plan A is not your permanent diet, but is a corrective diet to lower your pressure and, in some cases, cholesterol, triglycerides, to raise HDL, as well as to heal angina and other heart problems. It is important that you discuss your meals every time you visit the doctor. Keeping a food diary has been shown to help people lose weight more successfully and is strongly recommended. If you cannot lose weight on this diet, correction of your brain's chemistry and metabolism is necessary. Once this is corrected with medicine and nutrients, everyone can lose weight. A great deal of much obesity is neurological.

General Consideration of Foods Permitted

Your diet must be made up exclusively of wholesome foods, 100 percent pure, contain no additives, sugar, starch, fillers, and if possible, no preservatives. Specifically, you need food containing concentrated amounts of polyunsaturated oils (this is get-well ingredient number one); potassium, magnesium, calcium, B6, zinc, fats and protein to keep the health of your heart and blood pressure on target.

Protein or Animal Foods. Large amounts of fish, chicken, turkey and lesser amounts of beef, veal and pork are allowed unless sugar, MSG, corn syrup, corn starch, flour, pickling nitrates, or other preservatives are used in preparation. Have fish daily, even twice daily if you can. You need a minimum of 50 grams of protein on either Plan A or Plan B. Meet your needs with fish as well as with lean meats and some dairy foods if you are following Plan B. The best choices include mackerel, sardines, bluefish, salmon, snapper, halibut and trout. (Shellfish is a cause of hepatitis, and is lacking in Omega-3.)

Grains. White flours or refined carbohydrates are like sugar and have to be avoided, as well as bread, crackers and pasta, if you need to lose weight. Whole grains can be used, including matzoth, kasha, oats, brown rice and millet. Have 4 to 8 ounces on Plan B, but none on Plan A.

Cheese. Use hard or semisoft, aged yellow cheese. Examples are: Swiss, Cheddar, Brie, Camembert, blue, mozzarella, Gruyère, and goat. Avoid all diet cheeses, cheese spreads and cheese food substitutes such as Velveeta. You may have 1 to 2 ounces per day on Plan A, 4 ounces on Plan B. (These amounts apply to both, to aged and fresh cheese.)

Fresh Cheeses. Cottage, farmer, pot, ricotta, tofu and Monterey Jack. These cheeses contain more carbohydrates and may need greater restriction in obese patients.

Beverages. It is important when you have high blood pressure not to drink excessive amounts of water. Spring water and mineral water are preferred to tap water. Tangy club soda or herbal teas can be helpful. All herbal teas should be free of caffeine, sugar, barley, orange peel or aromatic herbs which may stimulate appetite. Decaffeinated coffee, which is ulcerogenic, is permitted (up to three cups). No caffeine sources are permitted—tea, regular coffee, etc.—which raise blood pressure. Diet soda use is sometimes necessary for reduction of appetite for sweets, but only temporarily. A glass of fruit juice can be substituted for a piece of fruit, if weight loss is not a problem. Vegetable juices can be made fresh. Lemon and lime juice can be used with no-salt seltzer and Nutrasweet to make lemonade. Make your own diet seltzers or sodas by adding fruit juice and nutrients.

Fruit. Restricting fruit can be useful in a low-carbohydrate diet for weight loss and reducing triglycerides, yet not for long. Fruit is high in potassium and helps prevent strokes, night cramps and heart arrhythmia. (Melons result in the least amount of weight gain.) Pears, apples, bananas and grapefruit are the best fruits to use. Oranges have too much sugar. Plan A: ½ to 1 fruit per day (if no weight loss occurs, you may not need to stop fruit consumption); Plan B: 1 to 5 fruits. One serving fruit juice equals 1 or 2 fruits.

Salad vegetables. Leafy greens, lettuce, escarole, romaine, parsley, collards, endive, spinach, mushrooms, cucumber, celery, radishes, peppers and bean sprouts. Plan A: 2 cups; Plan B: 2–4 cups.

Permissible Vegetables. Asparagus, broccoli, string or wax beans, cabbage, beet greens, cauliflower, chard, eggplant, kale, kohlrabi, mushrooms, tomato, onion, spinach, peppers, summer squash, zucchini, squash, okra, pumpkin, turnips, avocado, bamboo shoots, bean sprouts, water chestnuts, snow pea pods. Plan A: 4 to 7 oz. steamed or fresh vegetables; Plan B: 4 to 16 oz. steamed or fresh vegetables.

Nuts and Seeds. Nuts and seeds are generally avoided by hypertensives, although sunflower seeds (a rare treat on Plan A if unsalted), almonds, English walnuts and pecans are less fatty and somewhat tolerable, while pistachios and cashews are very poor choices. Very small servings (⅛ cup) from time to time are acceptable on Plan B only.

Dairy Products. These are high in carbohydrates, e.g., yogurt, buttermilk and milk. You may have 4 to 8 ounces per day of low-fat milk products on Plan B, but none on Plan A.

Spring Water. Use only spring water because your water supply may be contaminated by lead and may have excess copper from your plumbing.

Salt Substitute. Use potassium salt substitutes that contain only potassium chloride or magnesium chloride, not "light salt."

Alcohol. No more than one drink a day on Plan B, but none on Plan A.

Fats and Oils. Because cholesterol and triglycerides are fats, good fats and oils have a particular role in cleaning out the bad fats and oils. For those who have high blood pressure, safflower, sunflower and linseed oils lower blood pressure best because they work as diuretics. You may need 2 to 3 tablespoons per day. However, if you are on Plan B, you may have 1 tablespoon per day of Hain Safflower Mayonnaise (available in health food stores) in place of liquid safflower oil. If you have high cholesterol as well, add olive oil too, which lowers cholesterol better. You may need 1 tablespoon per day. Avoid saturated fat (including mayonnaise, cream, butter, etc.). Oil can be used with vinegar, adding grated cheese and mustard (contains salt) in small quantities, or try my hypertension shake.

Special Topics

The **egg** isn't such a bad egg. On my program, you can eat up to seven a week (in some cases, 14 on Plan A for vegetarians). Here's why: Egg intake is a minor factor in determining serum cholesterol levels. Egg consumption in the United States has steadily declined in the past few decades in an attempt to regulate serum cholesterol. It's an unfortunate omission because your total diet—the quantity and quality of fats, protein, carbohydrates and other foods you take in—is usually what determines your total serum cholesterol. In addition, the egg is a very valuable source of nutrition for very few calories. They provide top-quality protein, are low in fat, rich in protein and cancer fighting vitamin A, low in calories, rich in vitamin B12, plus various B vitamins and trace elements. Eggs are not only an acceptable food, but an essential, valuable one to a nutritionally well-planned diet and supplemental program.

Serum cholesterol levels beyond 200 appear to pose a major cardiovascular risk factor. To date, there have been many conflicting reports, but the most recent studies do not indicate a significant positive correlation between egg consumption and cholesterol levels. Neither does my firsthand work with patients.

Here is a typical study: 168 volunteers consumed a reduced fat-diet with an increased polyunsaturated-to-saturated fat ratio. One-half of the group received two eggs per week, while the other half had seven (high eggs). After four weeks, there was no significant rise in serum cholesterol levels with high egg consumption, probably due to the decrease in saturated fat intake. A one-year trial showed serum cholesterol correlated to fat consumption and *not* dietary cholesterol in eggs, as most would have expected. Did you know that a 100-

milligram cholesterol intake per day only raises your serum cholesterol by an insignificant 4 mg per day? Dietary *saturated* fatty acids are the main culprits (along with refined carbohydrates) in serum cholesterol elevation, not dietary cholesterol. And any rise in cholesterol due to egg consumption can be reduced by a diet high in polyunsaturates. My egg-eating hypertensives generally have a reduction in cholesterol due to the supplements of fish oil (EPA), primrose oil, polyunsaturates and niacin. Cholesterol levels usually decrease on my diet without eliminating eggs. Stress reduction is also an important factor.

Food Target Charts

Eliminated from the diet are the foods which I have found to do the most to create hypertension. In place of these substitute the foods I have found to help the most to reverse high blood pressure. They appear for easy reference in the food target charts that follow. Your goal is to reduce the amount of foods in Chart C and to phase out the foods in Chart A in favor of those in Chart B.

CHART A: THE TOP HYPERTENSION-MAKING FOODS

Alcohol	Pork
Salted food	Salted nuts
White flour	Pickled foods
Sugar	Smoked foods
Cakes and pastries	

CHART B: THE TOP HYPERTENSION-BREAKING FOODS

Fresh fish, e.g. snapper, halibut, salmon	Celery
	Salads and salad dressing
Fresh vegetables	Fruits

CHART C: FOODS PERMITTED OCCASIONALLY
if used sparingly (on Plan B, not Plan A)

Margarine, unsalted. (Hain safflower oil margarine is a wise choice—available at health food stores. Always make sure liquid oil is listed first).

Sour cream mayonnaise—use only "lite" or fat-reduced types.

Nuts and seeds—sunflower seeds, almonds, pecans are preferred over other less nutritious or higher in fat types (a small handful).

Diet sodas—preferably those sweetened without saccharin.

Dried fruits (small handful, at most).

Starchy vegetables—potatoes, corn, parsnips, etc.

Buttermilk, low-fat milk.

Peanut butter and other nut spreads if unsalted (use two times weekly, no more than 2 tablespoons at a time).

Red meat (use once a week).

Sample Menus:
Plan A

(For the hypertension patient who is overweight)

SAMPLE MENU DAY #1

Breakfast

One apple or pear, baked, with 1 tablespoon safflower oil, sliced and broiled with cinnamon.
1 soft-boiled or poached egg.
1 cup TONIC TEA* or 1 cup sugar-free fruit juice.

*Recipes for CAPITALIZED menu items may be located by consulting the index.

Lunch

4 to 6 oz. warm sardines with 1 tablespoon TWO-HERB PESTO or dash of light soy sauce, on lettuce.
¾ cup steamed broccoli-onion ring salad with garlic safflower oil dressing.
TONIC TEA (see recipes), or 1 cup HYPERTENSION SHAKE.

Snack

2 oz. cheese.

Dinner

1 cup TWO-WAY TOTAL HEALTH SALAD or
TUNA KEBABS.
Tossed salad.
Decaf or herb tea.

SAMPLE MENU DAY #2

Breakfast

½ sliced pink grapefruit; 1 tsp. NutraSweet.
1 poached egg on fresh spinach leaves.
Decaf or herb tea.

Lunch

Complete meal of watercress salad (cress, romaine lettuce, grated carrots and celery).
1 hard-boiled egg or 3-5 oz. tuna (olive oil and vinegar).
2 slices Swiss cheese.
½ cup mixed sprouts with 2 Tbsp. safflower oil, grated cheese and vinegar.
Mineral water, plain or flavored.

Snack

1 oz. natural Cheddar.

Dinner

4-6 oz. broiled or baked red snapper fillet, 1 Tbsp. TWO-HERB PESTO.

1 cup chicory or escarole salad with cold green beans or peas. Low-cal, low-sodium French dressing with 1 Tbsp. safflower oil.

1 cup sugar-free Jell-O.

Decaf or herb tea.

SAMPLE MENU DAY #3

Breakfast

Omelet (2 eggs, chopped onion, celery, pepper, salmon optional).

5 oz. tomato juice.

Lunch

Large piece of baked chicken (two pieces if really hungry). Spinach salad with a dressing made of 2 Tbsp. olive oil, basil, dill and a splash of vinegar.

Snack

HYPERTENSION SHAKE.

Dinner

4-6 oz. broiled salmon steak or other fish.

Steamed broccoli.

No-salt seltzer with lemon.

½-1 apple.

SAMPLE MENU DAY #4

Breakfast

2 health-food turkey imitation sausage.

½ grapefruit.

2 oz. cottage cheese or yogurt.

Lunch

6 oz. canned salmon with herbs, salt substitute.
1 cup of salad vegetables with lemon juice.

Snack

HYPERTENSION SHAKE (see recipes).

Dinner

Caesar salad with 1 boiled egg.
Spinach, celery, carrots.
2 oz. hard cheese.
4 oz. turkey.

SAMPLE MENU DAY #5

Breakfast

1 pear, sliced.
1-egg omelet with 2 oz. cheese.
Vegetables of your choice.
1 cup of herb tea.

Lunch

1 bowl chicken soup (made without rice, grains, potatoes or fat).
2 oz. cottage cheese or yogurt.
1 NutraSweet soft drink (water is preferable).
Optional large salad with safflower oil dressing mixes.

Dinner

4-6 oz. lean steak.
4 oz. steamed green beans with 1 Tbsp. safflower oil with seasonings.
½ cup salad vegetables with a dressing of 1-2 Tbsp. safflower oil and a dash of garlic and Parmesan cheese.

SAMPLE MENU DAY #6

Breakfast

1 low-fat piece of ham, warmed, not fried.
½-1 baked apple.
1 warm drink (decaf coffee or tea).

Lunch

4-6 oz. turkey (no nitrates).
1 cup steamed vegetables.

Dinner

1½ cups VEGETABLE CASSEROLE (chopped broccoli, cauliflower, onions, topped with grated cheese and baked).
Diet ginger ale.
2 cups SALAD with safflower oil dressing.

Sample Menus: Plan B

(For the hypertension patient who is at or near goal weight)

SAMPLE MENU DAY #1

Breakfast

2 BUCKWHEAT PANCAKES, or waffles with 1 Tbsp. melted BETTER BUTTER or 1 tsp. warm safflower or soy oil.

Lunch

6 oz. mackerel or bluefish fillets broiled with olive or safflower oil.
1-2 cups tossed greens with TANGY CUCUMBER DRESSING.
1 cup salt-free lemon seltzer or FRESH START TOMATO JUICE.

Snack

½ pita bread with HEALTHY HEART SPREAD or
2-4 oz. low-fat cottage cheese.

Dinner

4-6 oz. broiled chicken (broiled without skin).
½–1 cup steamed Brussels sprouts or turnips with safflower
oil and 2 to 4 oz. grated hard cheese.
Carrot, celery or cucumber sticks with lemon-pepper or salt
substitute.
TONIC TEA or decaffeinated espresso or coffee.

SAMPLE MENU DAY #2

Breakfast

Cup of fresh or frozen grapefruit sections with toasted wheat
germ sprinkles or toasted sunflower seeds.
2 scrambled eggs (use nonstick pan or pan spray) with chives
or onions or dill weed, Tabasco.
1 slice whole-wheat or rye toast.
1 cup carob cocoa or sugar-free cocoa.

Lunch

4-6 oz. canned salmon (diced green onion, minced garlic,
chopped celery) on spinach or lettuce leaves, with 1 Tbsp.
safflower oil, mayonnaise or plain yogurt.
1 whole-wheat matzo or 1 rice cake.
1 low-salt dill pickle, or fresh mushroom slices with paprika-
garlic powder.
1 cup low-sodium tomato juice or FRESH START TO-
MATO JUICE.

Snack

1 cup fresh or frozen strawberries or blueberries, or
1 cup HYPERTENSION SHAKE, any flavor.

Dinner

HAVE-IT-YOUR-WAY FILLET SOUFFLÉ or safflower-broiled flounder.
Baked potato with 1 Tbsp. plain yogurt.
Flavored seltzer (no salt) water with lemon slices.
Iced herb tea or decaf.

SAMPLE MENU DAY #3

Breakfast

1 slice whole-wheat toast.
1 poached egg.
Decaf drink.

Lunch

Roast turkey on whole-grain roll.
Small amount of safflower margarine or mayonnaise.
Celery sticks.
Diet soda.

Snack

2 oz. Brie cheese.

Dinner

6 oz. lean steak, broiled.
8 oz. steamed broccoli.
1 fruit of your choice.

SAMPLE MENU DAY #4

Breakfast

1 bowl whole-grain cereal (if sweetened, only with fruit juices—get at health food stores).
½ grapefruit.
Decaf drink.

Lunch

Caesar salad with 2 boiled eggs.
Dressing of 2 Tbsp. olive oil, splash of vinegar, herbs.

Snack

2 oz. sunflower seeds, or sunflower butter on whole-wheat crackers.

Dinner

Baked chicken (6 oz. or so).
6 oz. steamed green beans.
6 oz. cooked greens (e.g., spinach, kale).
No-salt seltzer.
1 pear.

SAMPLE MENU DAY #5

Breakfast

½ melon.
2 oz. hard cheese.
1 glass FRESH START TOMATO JUICE.

Lunch

Salad brought from home with greens, peppers, chives.
4 oz. tuna fish.
Low-calorie dressing.

Snack

HYPERTENSION SHAKE.

Dinner

Stir-fried vegetables with pieces of chicken.
Brown rice.
No-salt lemon seltzer.

SAMPLE MENU DAY #6

Breakfast

4 oz. yogurt.
1 Tbsp. *all-fruit* spread in yogurt.
Decaf drink.

Lunch

Slices of chicken on crisp bread.
1 Tbsp. safflower mayonnaise.
Lettuce, tomato.

Dinner

Broiled haddock.
1 Tbsp. olive oil on steamed vegetables.
1 medium potato.

SAMPLE MENU DAY #7

Breakfast

2-egg omelet (with chopped onion, celery, peppers and salmon).
2 rice cakes.

Lunch

Sliced lean beef on whole-grain roll.
Lettuce, tomato.

Dinner

Whole-grain tacos with salad vegetables, small amount of beans, 2-4 oz. cheese.
Brown rice (1 cup or so).
Diet soda.

Recipes: Juices

FRESH-START TOMATO JUICE

(Made from scratch—near zero-sodium thirst quencher)

12 large red ripe tomatoes (about 8 lb.), peeled and cored*

1 celery heart with leaves*

1 small yellow onion, peeled and sliced*

¼ tsp. dill seed

2 strips carefully scrubbed orange peel

Salt substitute or Tabasco to taste

Freshly ground white or black pepper to taste

Chop tomatoes and celery. Place with their juices in a large nonreactive kettle over high heat. (Porcelain or stainless steel are good; avoid aluminum cookware, as it is toxic.)

Add remaining ingredients and bring to a boil. Reduce heat and simmer 20 minutes, stirring occasionally to prevent scorching.

Strain mixture into a large bowl and purée remaining pulp in a blender or food processor.

Strain purée into bowl with juice. Mix well and transfer everything to a container with spout. Refrigerate, and for maximum nutrition and taste, finish in 5 days.

Makes 2 quarts.

NOTE: Contains less than 20 mg sodium per 6-ounce serving. Commercial canned tomato juice contains 550 mg per serving.

* Hypertension-breaking ingredient

Recipes: Spreads

BETTER BUTTER

Blend ½ stick of soft, whipped, no-salt vegetable margarine with ½ cup regular or high-oleic* safflower, corn or peanut oil, or pure olive oil.* For additional vitamins B and E and better spreadability, add the contents of one 400 mg vitamin E capsule* and 1 Tbsp. high-potency soy lecithin granules (available at health stores). Blend well. Spoon into a butter dish or margarine tub and refrigerate.

* Hypertension-breaking ingredient

Recipes: Drinks

HYPERTENSION SHAKE
(Plan B only)

1 package soft drained tofu

1½ cups any fruit such as bananas, papayas, etc.

Natural sweetener (optional)

Spices: your choice—cinnamon, nutmeg, lemon juice, vanilla

Bottled water or skim milk if needed

In a blender or food processor, combine all ingredients and whip until smooth.

NOTE: Frozen fruits may be substituted for fresh.

Variation #1: for VEGETABLE HYPERTENSION SHAKE, omit sweetener and spices and substitute any hypertension-breaking vegetable. Add 1 teaspoon olive oil for high cholesterol and salt substitute to taste.

For SUPER HYPERTENSION AND CHOLESTEROL-BREAKING SHAKE, add 2-3 Tbsp. of safflower oil.

* Hypertension-breaking ingredient

HYPERTENSION SHAKES **Low-Carbohydrate Diet—Plan A**
Make in a blender: 3¼ cups crushed ice 2-3 Tbsp. safflower oil (as directed) ½ banana NutraSweet to taste Dash of nonalcoholic fruit or vanilla extract (available through health food stores)
Make in a blender: 2-3 Tbsp. safflower oil as directed ⅔ cups frozen fruit (preferably melon or apple or a banana that has been frozen ahead of time) 3-4 ice cubes NutraSweet to taste NOTE: Have no other carbohydrates on days you choose this shake.

HYPERTENSION SHAKES
Complex Carbohydrate Diet—Plan B
(Normal Weight)

Make in a blender:

2-3 Tbsp. safflower oil (as directed)

1 small-medium banana

5 oz. low-fat milk (less for Plan A)

NutraSweet to taste

NOTE: If you choose this version, have little additional carbohydrate that day.

Make in a blender:

4 oz. soy milk (Vitasoy is a good brand)

½ cups crushed ice

½ banana

2-3 Tbsp. safflower oil (as directed)

Dash of nonalcoholic fruit or vanilla extract (available through health food stores)

HYPERTENSION SHAKE
Complex Carbohydrate Diet—Plan B
(Underweight)

3 Tbsp. safflower oil

1 large banana

6 oz. low-fat milk

NutraSweet to taste

Dash of nonalcoholic vanilla or fruit extract

Recipes: Fish

CHINESE STEAMED FISH KEBABS WITH CASHEWS

12 oz. swordfish or 16 oz. halibut steak, ¾-inch thick*

2 tsp. reduced-sodium soy sauce

1 tsp. lemon juice

1 tsp. safflower or olive oil*

1 clove garlic, minced

⅛ tsp. red pepper*

2 green onions with tops, cut into thin 1-inch strips*

2 tsp. thinly sliced cashews or almonds

2 Tbsp. minced cilantro (Chinese parsley)*

Rinse fish; pat dry. Cut into serving portions. Combine next 5 ingredients in a small bowl; set aside. Boil water in bottom half of steamer. A steam cooker is ideal, but any deep saucepan or electric skillet with a tight-fitting lid will work. (Improvise by setting a wire rack on empty tuna cans, tops and bottoms removed, inside saucepan.) Arrange fish on top rack of steamer; brush with soy sauce mixture.

Scatter green onions on top of fish.

Position fish over boiling water and cover steamer tightly. Steam 5 to 6 minutes until fish is opaque. Using a spatula, transfer fish to serving platter. Sprinkle with cashews and garnish with cilantro.

Two servings. Preparation time: 15 minutes. Cooking time: 10 minutes.

178 calories per serving; 25 grams protein (59% of calories); 7 grams fat (35%); 48 mg cholesterol; 253 mg sodium; 470 mg potassium.

* Hypertension-breaking ingredient

TUNA KEBABS

1 lb. fresh tuna steak cut into 1 × 1 inch squares

2 Tbsp. chopped garlic

1 Tbsp. chopped ginger root

1 cup safflower oil

½ cup tamari soy sauce,* low sodium

8 cherry tomatoes

1 small onion cut into quarters

Dice tuna and marinate in remaining ingredients except tomatoes and onion.

Drain and alternate tuna, tomato, onion on skewers.

Cook on hot outdoor grill or indoor hibachi approximately 5 minutes on each side.

Two to three generous servings.

Variation: Leave tuna in steaks and marinate tuna steak undiced. Grill 7-10 minutes each side.

Any firm-flesh fish may be substituted (e.g., halibut, salmon, swordfish).

Leftovers make tasty tuna salads for lunch.

*If you have a wheat allergy, use nonwheat tamari sauce, available at health food stores.

HAVE-IT-YOUR-WAY FILLET SOUFFLÉ

1 lb. sole or flounder, filleted

¼ cup Monterey Jack cheese, grated; ¼ cup mild Cheddar, grated

5 egg whites

2-3 Tbsp. poaching liquid

1 cup plain nonfat yogurt

¼ cup whole-wheat bread crumbs (optional)

Poach fish 4 minutes in hot water (not boiling); remove and flake. Reserve 2-3 Tbsp. hot liquid.

Beat egg whites until they form stiff peaks; set aside. Combine grated cheese, yogurt and poaching liquid with flaked fish, then fold into egg whites. Pour into baking dish. (Optional: sprinkle ¼ cup whole-wheat bread crumbs on top.) Bake in 350-degree oven for 35 minutes.

NOTE: If available, use reduced-fat, reduced-sodium cheese. Variation: Substitute turbot or catfish for either the sole or flounder.

Recipes: Appetizers, Dressing, Side Dishes

JICAMA-CHILI PEPPER RELISH

1 medium jicama, about 1 pound*
1 large carrot*
1 medium zucchini*
1 pickled chilpotle pepper in an adobo sauce with liquid*
1 cup finely chopped onion*
4 garlic cloves, peeled and minced*
1 bay leaf
6 whole black peppercorns
½ cup water
⅓ cup olive oil*
1 Tbsp. chopped cilantro or parsley*
1 tsp. good quality dried oregano

Using a knife, remove skin from jicama. Cut into half-inch dice. Place in a bowl. Peel carrot. Steam cook. Cut into half-inch dice. Add to the bowl with jicama. Scrub and trim the zucchini. Cut into half-inch dice, add to the bowl.

Drain the chilpotles, reserving the pickling sauce (one chili makes a relatively mild marinade; use 2 if desired). Cut chilies open lengthwise, scrape out the seeds. Finely chop and place in a separate, medium-sized bowl.

Add onion, garlic, bay leaf, peppercorns, vinegar, water, olive oil and cilantro or parsley to chilpotle in bowl. Blend in the reserved chilpotle sauce. Crumble oregano and add to bowl. Whisk all the ingredients together and pour the marinade over jicama mixture. Toss with the marinade to coat completely.

Boil. Cook 10-12 minutes until tender. Drain.

Return vegetables to pan, add yogurt or ricotta and oil.

Mash ingredients until coarse. Add remaining seasonings, blend thoroughly and serve warm.

Makes 4 servings.

Variation: Substitute carrots or celery root for parsnips; use Jerusalem artichokes in place of potatoes to reduce starch.

* Hypertension-breaking ingredient

TANGY CUCUMBER DRESSING

(All-purpose low sodium, high-potassium dressing)

1 12-oz. cucumber, pared, seeded and coarsely chopped*

½ cup parsley sprigs*

¼ cup plain nonfat yogurt

1 scallion with top, sliced*

1 Tbsp. tarragon vinegar

1 Tbsp. Dijon-style mustard

1 clove garlic, sliced*

½ tsp. celery seed

½ tsp. dried dillweed*

Few drops Worcestershire sauce

Place all ingredients in blender and process until smooth. Refrigerate several hours to blend flavors. Makes 1 cup. Preparation time: 10 minutes plus refrigeration time.

A perfect complement to the tanginess of mustard greens, cabbage, as well as fresh spinach and tender greens. May be used as a dip for other vegetable or crackers. NOTE: Refrigerated, keeps one week.

15 calories per 2 Tbsp. serving; 2 grams fat (13% of calories); 4 mg cholesterol; 34 mg sodium; 114 mg potassium.

* Hypertension-breaking ingredient

POTATO AND PARSNIP PURÉE
(Plan B only)

1½ lbs. russet potatoes, about 4*

2 large parsnips, trimmed and scraped, sliced crosswise (about 2 cups worth)*

1 large yellow onion, peeled and sliced*

Salt substitute to taste

½ cup thick yogurt, yogurt cheese or ricotta (low-fat)*

Pinch of nutmeg; freshly ground pepper to taste

½ cup chives (or any herb of your choice)

Peel and quarter potatoes (you should have about 3 to 3½ cups).

Combine potatoes with onion and parsnips and garlic in large saucepan. Add water to cover, add salt substitute and bring to a boil.

Cook 10-12 minutes until tender. Drain.

Return vegetables to pan, add yogurt or ricotta and oil. Mash ingredients until coarse. Add remaining seasonings, blend thoroughly and serve warm.

Makes 4 servings.

Variation: Substitute carrots or celery root for parsnips; use Jerusalem artichokes in place of potatoes to reduce starch.

* Hypertension-breaking ingredient

TWO-STEP, TWO-HERB PESTO
(50% lower in fat and sodium)

8 shelled Brazil nuts

¼ cup grated or ¼ cup of Asiago* or low-fat Parmesan cheese*

2 cloves garlic, crushed*

½ cup pure safflower oil

1½ cups fresh parsley, chopped, stems included*

½ cups fresh basil, chopped, stems included*

Tabasco sauce or potassium salt substitute to taste*

1 to 2 Tbsp. boiling water

Put nuts, cheese and garlic in blender. Cover and start machine. Add oil in a thin stream, blending until mixture is smooth. Add herbs a few sprigs at a time. Season with Tabasco or potassium substitute.

With blender running, add boiling water to bring mixture to a mayonnaise-like consistency. Makes 4 servings.

NOTE: Change the nut and the cheese and you can put this traditionally high-fat high-sodium sauce back on the menu. Eight Brazil nuts supply half the fat of the usual ⅓ cup of pine nuts. And Asiago (a Parmesan-like grating cheese carried by better supermarkets) has 75% less fat than conventional grating cheeses.

* Hypertension-breaking ingredient

HEALTHY HEART SPREAD

1 medium size eggplant

1 small onion, finely chopped or grated

3 Tbsp. sugar-free, salt-free safflower oil mayonnaise

Tabasco to taste

Peel eggplant and slice.

Bake at 375 degrees approximately 30 minutes. Dice and purée by hand or in a food processor until smooth. Fold in mayonnaise, onion and Tabasco.

Delicious as a pita bread spread, filling or cracker dip.

Variation: Add 1-2 cloves, mashed, minced garlic, or one finely chopped fresh tomato.

Recipes: Salads

TWO-WAY TOTAL HEALTH SALAD

Salad Base

¼ cup pure extra-virgin olive oil or ¼ cup safflower oil

2 Tbsp. herb vinegar

Pepper and salt substitute to taste

⅓ cup thinly sliced green onions

2 crushed and diced garlic cloves*

Salad A with Herbs

¼ cup finely minced fresh parsley

¼ cup finely minced fresh tarragon

1 Tbsp. minced fresh dill

1 Tbsp. minced celery leaves

½ lb. green snap beans, steamed and cooled, in 1-inch lengths

2 hard-boiled eggs, coarsely chopped

Salad B with Seafood

¼ cup finely chopped fresh basil

¼ cup finely chopped fresh chervil

½ cup finely diced fresh celery

1-1½ cups cooked salmon, mackerel or trout* in bite-sized chunks

3 cups mixed salad greens*

Combine salad base ingredients. Mix Salad A or B.

Whisk oil with vinegar, salt substitute, pepper and combine base with Salad A or B. Mix well, marinate at least 30 minutes before serving.

Makes 6 to 8 servings. Refrigerated, keeps 3–4 days.

* Hypertension-breaking ingredient

Recipes: Teas

Here are the twelve herb teas that can significantly affect
your blood pressure because they are rich in heart and artery
health minerals, trace elements and vitamins. Sip 1 to 2 cups
of any of the below singly or in combination daily. For dou-
ble-your-pleasure benefits, look for blends that combine two or
more herbs. They are available at health food stores and coffee/
tea shops and mail-order herb companies.

Crampbark	Mistletoe	Scullcap	Ginger
Hawthorne	Capsicum	Hops	Barberry
Valerian	Parsley	Passionflower	Comfrey

HYPERTENSION LEMONADE

7 tsp. lemon or lime juice

No-salt seltzer

NutraSweet to taste

Chapter 3

Nine Success Tips for Eating Out

1. Food for your heart can be wonderful, not wimpy; hearty as well as healthy, even if you aren't in the kitchen calling the shots. Here's how to sneak 25 percent of the fat out of your next meal out. On the right is a typical American meal which derives over 40 percent of its calories from fat. On the left is a just-as-filling alternative with 50 percent less fat, one-fourth the cholesterol, and five or more of the top hypertension-breaking ingredients per selection. And any "white-cloth" restaurant will whip it up for you at your request.

TYPICAL PLAN A	TYPICAL PLAN B
25% protein 15% fat 60% complex carbohydrate	70% protein 20% fat 10% complex carbohydrate
For example:	For example:
½ cup tossed salad: romaine lettuce, grated carrot, sliced cucumber, red cabbage 2 Tbsp. grated low-fat cheese 1 Tbsp. olive oil 4 to 6 oz. tuna fish in salad 1 cup decaf coffee or tea with skim milk ½ cantaloupe or berries in season	1 cup onion soup 3½ oz. tenderloin steak, broiled 1 baked potato 1 Tbsp. sour cream ½ cup green beans almondine with butter Lettuce wedge (⅙ head) 1 Tbsp. Russian dressing 1 cup decaffeinated coffee with cream

2. Saving on sodium is just as easy. Here are eleven ways to cut down on salt without cutting it out. The right-hand column indicates the milligrams of sodium avoided.

Instead of	Substitute	Saved
Bologna, 3 oz. (872 mg sodium)	Beef, 3 oz. roast (50)	822
Butter, 1 Tbsp. lightly salted (116 mg sodium)	Butter, 1 Tbsp. unsalted (2)	114
Cheese, 1 oz. provolone (248 mg sodium)	Cheese, 1 oz. Swiss (74)	174
Clams, hard-shell, 3½ oz. shelled (205 mg sodium)	Clams, soft-shell, 3½ oz. shelled (36)	169
Garlic salt, 1 tsp. (1850 mg sodium)	Garlic powder, 1 tsp. (1)	1849
Kidney beans, 1 cup canned (844 mg sodium)	Kidney beans, 1 cup home-cooked from dry (4)	840
Oatmeal, 1 envelope instant, ¾ cup cooked (400 mg sodium)	Oatmeal, ¾ cup cooked, old-fashioned or quick (0)	400
Olives, 3 green (242 mg sodium)	Olives, 3 ripe black (96)	146
Sauerkraut, 1 cup, drained (1121 mg sodium)	Cabbage, 1 cup cooked, shredded (29)	1092
Shrimp, 3 oz., drained, canned (1955 mg sodium)	Shrimp, 3 oz., fresh (140)	1815
Soy sauce, 1 Tbsp. (892 mg sodium)	Teriyaki sauce, 1 Tbsp. (630)	262

3. Here are 20 swaps to save on lunch-counter calories that add hypertension-boosting pounds. The right-hand column shows the number of calories avoided.

Instead of	Substitute	Cal.
1 bagel (3½ oz.)	1 whole-wheat English muffin	60
1 slice whole-wheat bread	1 very thin slice multigrain bread	30
4 oz. cheeseburger	4 oz. hamburger	80
½ fried chicken breast with skin	½ roast chicken breast without skin	80
1 cup beef chow mein or chop suey with noodles	1 cup chicken chow mein or chop suey with noodles	120
1 cup New England clam chowder	1 cup Manhattan clam chowder	70
12 oz. regular cola	12 oz. diet cola	159
1 cup corn kernels	1 cup broccoli spears	90
1 Tbsp. blue cheese dressing	1 Tbsp. low-calorie Italian dressing	70
1 beef frankfurter	1 turkey frankfurter	45
12 oz. frozen regular lasagna	12 oz. frozen reduced-calorie lasagna	250
1 cup whole milk	1 cup low-fat (1%) milk	50
1 cup apple juice	1 apple	50
1 Tbsp. peanut butter	1 Tbsp. jam (fruit only)	40
1 baked potato with skin	1 baked potato w/o skin	75
1 flour tortilla	1 corn tortilla	65
3 oz. oil-packed tuna	3 oz. water-packed tuna	30
1 waffle (7 inches)	2 pancakes (4 inches each)	85

4. Don't keep out of restaurants to keep your blood pressure down. Make the enemy woo you. Patronize the ones that offer fat-free, low-salt "spa" cuisine or ones that are willing to broil fish for you even if it's off the menu—and the calorie, fat and sodium trimming will already have been done for you.

5. If the dressing of the day is "creamy" anything, have vinaigrette on the side instead, or oil, vinegar or lemon.

6. Request seafood broiled "dry" or served with a vegetable oil, not butter. Have vegetables and brown rice steamed without salt. And remove all visible fat from meat and the skin from chicken and turkey.

7. Anything that's poached (eggs, fish, vegetables, fruit) is perfect, but pass up anything pickled or smoked or made with MSG or salt. If you're eating Oriental, call ahead and request that MSG and additional salt (soy sauce is very high in salt) be left out. Skip any dish made with lobster sauce.

8. The healthiest cold desserts are sugar-free Jell-O, sorbets, fruit ices or glazes. All are fat-free—and better restaurants may prepare them without sugar as well. Keep portions small. All but the Jell-O have carbohydrates, which can boost triglycerides and are suitable for Plan B only. Another good meal-ender: fresh berries or melon with low-fat *crème fraîche* in place of whipped cream. Better than cream: a no-calorie twist of fresh ginger root, a great heart-health maker. You will never miss the cream or sugar. Frozen bananas can be whipped in a food processor to make a sorbet-type dessert or smoothies, which are great—and great for the heart. Also try natural fruit popsicles. Stick with fruits as the sweetener.

9. If all the desserts are no-no's, request that your salad or extra vegetables be served in place of dessert, or ask for 2 oz. of hard cheese and ½ fruit.

Chapter 4

Putting the Whole Program Together

Ten-Step Daily Program

NOTE: Ideally, your physician should determine your daily dosage of vitamins and drugs. This is essential if you have high-risk hypertension. Here is a typical 10-step program.

1. Take designated a.m. supplements and medications (if any) with water, TONIC TEA, ANTIHYPERTENSION SHAKE* or fresh-squeezed juice.

2. Have your approved Braverman Program breakfast.

3. Do designated hypertension relief exercises, e.g., meditation, prayer, biofeedback, CES†at the level you or your doctor have chosen.

4. Take the designated midday supplements and drugs (if any).

5. Choose an approved lunch.

6. Take a stress-relief break, e.g., meditation, prayer, biofeedback, CES.

---

*Either can be used. The antihypertension shake will be more successful. Both drinks contribute to normalization of blood pressure and contain selected nutrients which protect you from the negative effects of any drugs you are taking.
†See also my books *What's Your Spiritual Health?* and *P.A.T.H. Wellness Manual.*

7. Take designated p.m. supplements.

8. Enjoy Braverman Program dinner.

9. Take pre-sleep supplements (if any).

10. Wake up refreshed, filled with energy and positive mood.

Typical Five-Step Plan for Eliminating Drugs in an Obese Hypertensive and Substituting Nutritional Supplements

(For Hypertensives on Plan B)

1. Blood tests, and possibly a stress test, and any other indicated tests are done by the physician. Start Plan A for weight loss 2 to 4 pounds the first week, e.g. high protein, vegetables, fish, safflower oil.

2. Initiate:
   - Up to 7 evening primrose oil, borage oil or black currant oil pills. (Evening primrose oil may be difficult to obtain. EPA-GLA is an alternative.)
   - 7 high-potency fish oil. (Or 3 tablespoons of high-potency, emulsified, liquid fish oil. Several flavors are available.)
   - 7 of Dr. Braverman's HTN multi (Formula #1, ingredients in Appendix).
   - 1 of Dr. Braverman's magnesium formula; adjust to bowel function—drop if bowels are loose, increase if constipated. The Calcium Formula also controls loose bowels.
   - 2 potassium chloride pills (10-20 meq) (approximately 900-1800milligrams).
   - 1 multivitamin with minerals—Dr. Braverman's formula preferred. Women should take calcium to prevent osteoporosis, especially if thin and fair-skinned or postmenopausal.

3. With doctor's supervision, immediately stop diuretic (unless Lasix or super-strong diuretic, then cut by ½ and taper off gradually). If no diuretic, cut beta-blocker to ½.
   - If angiotensin drug, reduce dosage by ½ or ⅓.
   - If calcium channel blocker, reduce by ½ or ⅓. If Aldomet, reduce and substitute for better medication.
   - See your doctor every 7 to 14 days for evaluation. Telephone doctor if any unpleasant side effects occur.
   - Reduce drugs gradually by ½ to ⅓ every 1 to 2 weeks.

   If blood pressure is not lowering fast, then traditionally add niacin. This is usually only necessary in patients who take 2 to 5 drugs for HTN. Increase fish oil, primrose oil and Formula #1 for difficult cases.

4. As weight loss progresses, the need for nutrients decreases once the drug is removed. Usually 1 to 2 drugs are stopped in 30 days. With a condition resistant to relaxation techniques, biofeedback and the brain-stress controller CES (see Chapter 12) should do the trick. Chelation is also another valuable alternative.

   And what if those high numbers for cholesterol and blood pressure don't drop? You can add on these next nutritional steps. Other nutrient options for difficult hypertension include:
   - Higher doses of HTN multi oils and less antioxidant.
   - Calcium, especially for women.
   - Coenzyme Q10 (CoQ10), especially if you have a history of heart trouble.
   - Arginine, especially if the cholesterol is high. There is also a new zero-flush niacin, inositol hexonicotinate, which is a breakthrough for niacin therapy, allowing high dosages. (Usually this niacin may be taken without side effects, but sometimes a partial flush occurs.)

5. Do only mild exercise in this phase. Concentrate on meditation (or prayer), with CES, stress reduction (see options on pp. 157) and light exercise.

Maintenance Program

Once your weight is normalized, shift to Plan B diet. Continue exercise, meditation (or prayer), and stress reduction.

See your doctor once every 30 days or as needed. Continue with nutrients in these amounts:

- 4 high-potency fish oil tablets (recommended: 2 tablespoons of Twin Labs super-potency liquid EPA).
- 4 primrose oil or borage oil capsules (borage oil is probably a better replacement for primrose oil).
- 1–2 Dr. Braverman's Multi.
- 1–3 Dr. Braverman's Magnesium.
- 1–3 Dr. Braverman's Calcium.
- 1 potassium chloride, or citrate 10 milliequivalents every day of potassium chloride milliequivalents.

What You Can Expect

Results in 30 to 90 days. Blood pressure in normal range. Normalization of triglycerides with up to 1700 percent decrease. Cholesterol below 200 or a 5 to 100 percent decrease in cholesterol, HDL above 40 (50 to 300 percent increase). Discontinuing 1 to 2 diuretics (unless severe congestive heart failure, etc.). Reduction or discontinuance of all beta-blockers. Liberalizing diet to Plan B in many cases.

Results in 90 to 180 days. Off most drugs unless you are taking 4 to 6 hypertension drugs. Cholesterol as low as 80 to 110, usually about 150 to 180. Low blood pressure, in some cases, if nutrients are not reduced.

Results in 6 months. Liberalizing diet to Plan B for all patients—with restrictions on carbohydrates for those remaining obese.

One year from today. Reduction in nutrients is needed to keep blood pressure down. Continued reduction of drugs if severe hypertension. Liberalizing diet. Drug-free, robust life with possibly less nutrients and an easy diet.

How to Make Supplement-Taking an Easier Pill to Swallow

■ Take all designated vitamins at one time either shortly before, during (especially well-tolerated), or after a meal, when they're digested with the greatest efficiency. To eliminate belching connected with fish oil capsules, take them *before* meals. No-flush or, better yet, zero-flush niacin taken *after* meals will produce a greater flush than if it's taken before meals. For severe flushing reactions, a baby aspirin helps relieve symptoms, or it can be dropped if a real problem. Nausea is an occasional side effect. If you have trouble swallowing vitamins, grind them to a powder in a blender or coffee mill and combine with any liquid or apple sauce; or better yet, take the Braverman Hypertension Formula, a multivitamin that combines most of the nutrients on your program into a single tablet (see Appendix).

■ Need a gadget to remind you it's pill time? Ask your pharmacist about the "Med-Tymer"—an electronic pill-container cap that sounds an alarm and flashes a light at medication time. Fits most medication bottles.

■ Refrigerate all oils.

■ Obtain a fishing tackle/lure type of compartmentalized plastic box, stock the compartments with a monthly supply of vitamins (with freshener), and thus reduce your vitamin-taking time to five minutes daily. This is an important tip for managing and simplifying your nutritional regimen. Particularly if you are of a flexible, fun-loving, artistic or romantic temperament, you will find it difficult to discipline yourself to follow the program.

Chapter 5

Nutritional Treatments for Hypertension*

Over the last fifteen years, medicine has gone through a revolutionary change. The medical dictum was that nutrition and lifestyle made no contribution to chronic disease. Medicine has done a complete turnaround and has started a war against bad lifestyle habits like smoking, fat consumption and sedentary behavior. Modern medicine has accepted its responsibility to direct the lifestyles of people toward health. Orthomolecular medicine was shouting like a voice in the wilderness before the rest of the profession identified the important role of nutrition. Although orthomolecular physicians and scientists first touted the important role of nutrition in mental health, mental health is actually now known to be the foundation for all health. Indirectly, and often directly, orthomolecular physicians and scientists have heralded the way for the complete nutrition revolution in the United States. This nutritional revolution is most evident in the transformation of the American doctor's treatment of hypertension. More than any other illness, it is now accepted by mainstream medicine that nutritional and dietary factors and therapies should be utilized by physicians in treating hypertension.

*Adapted from an article in *The Journal of Orthomolecular Medicine,* Fourth Quarter, 7:4, 1992.

EPIDEMIOLOGY

Hypertension is clinically defined as systolic blood pressure greater than 140 mmhg and/or diastolic blood pressure greater than 90 mmhg. It is a leading problem in the United States, where nearly 20 percent of Americans are affected by it. More than ten million Americans are being treated for this disease at a cost of over $2.5 billion, the largest medical expenditure for a single disease in the United States.

High blood pressure afflicts over 60 million Americans and contributes to one million deaths per year in the United States, adding $18 billion per year to United States health expenditures. Genetic, psychological, and environmental factors play a role in hypertension. In 1975, over half (54 percent) of all United States deaths were from cardiovascular disease. Hypertension is the most significant and preventable contributing factor. Hypertension is associated with an increased risk of heart failure, kidney failure and stroke. It is virtually an epidemic in the African-American population, where about one-third of blacks between 18 and 49 have hypertension and two-thirds of those over age 50 have hypertension. However, the ratio of black to white hypertensives is decreasing, probably due to better treatment of high blood pressure in blacks than in whites. African-Americans are twice as likely to suffer from kidney failure, and have the world's second highest incidence of stroke, behind the Japanese.

In addition to increasing incidence of stroke, high blood pressure appears as a contributing factor in some cancer deaths as well. Vigorous treatment of elevated blood pressure also reduces strokes. Another complication of hypertension is that it impairs nutrient absorption from the diet.

Hypertension is also an increasing problem among children, possibly due to dietary factors, such as high fat and refined carbohydrate consumption. Hypertension has been correlated to a diet high in calories, sodium, sodium/potassium ratio, alcohol, and low in protein, calcium, magnesium, micronutrients and vitamins. Hypertension increases with age and occurs more frequently in men. Women who get pregnant at a later age (35 or over) have increased complications, especially essential hypertension.

Five percent of all hypertension has been classified as "secondary," that is, associated with some other disease (usually renal or adrenocortical tumor). Ninety-five percent of hypertension is classified as "essential" hypertension, primarily related to stress, nutrition and other lifestyle-like factors. Most hypertension cases are probably due to arteriosclerosis.

Atherosclerosis formation is a very complex problem and may be related to an intracellular deficiency in essential fatty acids. One study suggests that there are four categories of hypertensive patients, each with a different pathophysiology and pharmacological profile: the young patient often has an increased cardiac output, the middle age patient's total peripheral resistance is elevated, the elderly patient's total peripheral resistance is even further increased while their intravascular volume is contracted, and obese and black patients have elevated total blood volume and cardiac output (Messerli, 1987).

TREATMENT

Nutritional treatment of essential hypertension is very successful and should be the first approach. A whole array of new symptoms and side effects manifest themselves with the usage of standard hypertensive pharmacological therapy, and any regimen for hypertension may have detrimental effects on the cerebral functioning of the aged. Approximately 30 to 50 percent of elderly patients experience side effects from antihypertensive therapy. Rapid treatment of hypertension in the elderly can cause quick drops in blood pressure and possibly lead to stroke. Antihypertensive drugs have been postulated to be related to the genesis of acute as well as chronic pancreatitis. Drug therapy for mild hypertension (systolic 140–150, diastolic 90–100) will only help a small percentage of patients, and the side effects may far outweigh the potential gain. Antihypertensive therapy should be matched to the underlying biochemical problems; this is more efficacious therapy than the standard stepped-care approach.

The financial cost of an antihypertensive regimen should also be considered in terms of long-term patient compliance. Labartho further supports the use of nonpharmacological therapy in mild hypertension while condemning drug use. The great many side effects of antihypertensive medications for treating mild hypertension has caused many cases of noncompliance and ineffective long-term therapy, doctors find. It is becoming apparent that drug regimens for the treatment of hypertension have become increasingly unsatisfactory to modern physicians. Even mild hypertension poses risks in the long run and should be treated. This is where our nutritional and lifestyle program has a tremendous input.

DRUGS AND THEIR DANGERS

Diuretics. There are approximately five categories of drug treatments: diuretics, beta-blockers, alpha-blockers, angiotensin-2 inhibitors and calcium channel blockers. The most commonly used treatment is diuretics, which continue to have a large variety of side effects. Patients who receive diuretics as their sole therapy have an increased risk of mortality due to myocardial infarction or sudden death. Also, diuretics deplete magnesium and potassium. Potassium-sparing diuretics can cause an excess of potassium in the blood when administered, while sodium loss can be a result of thiazide diuretic therapy. Thiazide diuretic therapy in the elderly leads to almost 50 percent of the patients displaying hypokalemia or hypomagnesemia, i.e., intracellular potassium magnesium loss. Dyckner and Wester demonstrated in 1983 that 42 percent of patients with arterial hypertension had subnormal levels of skeletal muscle magnesium. Potassium deficiency can usually be corrected, but the loss of magnesium is rarely addressed.

Diuretic drugs prescribed for hypertension cause glucose intolerance and raise glycohemoglobin concentrations as well as increase blood cholesterol and triglycerides. One study showed that with up to one year of treatment with diuretics, plasma cholesterol increased accordingly.

Beta-Blockers. The second most commonly used therapy is beta-blockers. Beta-blockers have similar side effects to diuretics. Undesirable serum lipid fractions have been found in patients treated with beta-blockers. At least 25 percent of all patients using beta-blockers will develop a need for antidepressants because these drugs can cause depression. This further complicates the issue because antidepressants are notorious for having their own undesirable side effects. Moreover, they can cause an increased risk of heart failure. Patients on beta-blockers had an increased risk of coronary heart attacks, as did patients on anticholesterol drugs or diuretics, other researchers have found.

Beta-blockers, like most antihypertensive drugs, can cause sexual dysfunction. Twenty-eight percent of patients on the beta-blocker timolol maleate experienced adverse reactions, most commonly fatigue, dizziness and nausea. Lipid-soluble beta-blockers that cross the blood brain barrier have been known to produce neurotoxic side effects as well as cold in the extremities. Some evidence indicates that beta-blockers are more effective in Caucasian than black hypertensives. Long-term use of beta-blockers, more than two to three years, is probably contraindicated for most patients.

Alpha-Blockers. Alpha-blockers such as Catapres have a significant number of side effects, notably hypotension, constipation, sedation, dry mouth, and dizziness. We have not found them to be particularly helpful in long-term treatment of hypertension.

Methyldopa and Angiotensin. Methyldopa seems to lower work performance and general well-being, as compared to other antihypertensive agents. Methyldopa was compared to Propranolol and Captopril and rated worse in causing the following conditions: fatigue, sexual disorder, headache, neck pressure, insomnia and nightmares. Up to 50 percent of patients on one of these three drugs experienced fatigue or lethargy; up to 30 percent had some form of sexual disorder; and over 10 percent had sleep disorder, nightmares, headaches, anxiety, irritability, palpitations, dry mouth, dizziness, nausea and muscle cramps. Captopril, an angiotensin inhibitor, is one of the safer drugs for hypertension, because it does not affect a patient's glucose tolerance. Nevertheless, angiotensin inhibitors seem to affect trace elements significantly. Selenium and zinc are decreased and copper increased, which may be a problem in the psychologically sensitive. Calcium channel blockers are seen to be more efficient and give fewer side effects, compared to the traditional hypertension therapy of diuretics and/or beta-blockers.

Vasodilators. The use of vasodilators like nitrates is frequently accompanied by headaches. Nitrates have been used for the treatment of angina pectoris and congestive heart failure, but have not been systematically studied for clinical usage in hypertension. Drugs like hydralazine also produce depression in 10 to 15 percent of the patients taking it. Dopamine-metabolite inhibitors (i.e., methyldopa or Aldomet) are frequently linked with depression and other negative side effects. Hence, we have found virtually all drug regimens have side effects significant enough to warrant searching for other modalities.

It has become evident that treating hypertension with drugs is not cost effective, given the current efficacy of drug regimens. Some researchers suggest that the treatment of mild hypertension may not be beneficial. Mild hypertensive patients have a diastolic blood pressure between 90 and 104. Over the age of 80, in particular, there seems to be little benefit from treating hypertension.

It appears that once drug regimens are opted for, drug therapies will spiral. However, the Framingham heart study indicates that only a certain small percentage of formerly treated hypertensives maintain normal blood pressure when treatment is stopped. After abrupt withdrawal from antihypertensives, blood pressure usually rebounds and the need for drugs continues to increase. This is why a suitable nutritional program is necessary. Ironically, the *Annals of Internal Medicine* and the *AMA News* have finally suggested that dietary changes and *not* drugs are the best option. The focus of treatment in hypertension should move towards elimination of pharmacological side effects and reduction of risk factors for coronary heart disease. A 1987 article in the *Journal of the American Medical Association* stated that "Nutritional therapy may substitute for drugs in a sizeable portion of hypertensives, and if drugs are still needed it can lessen some unwanted biochemical effects of drug treatment." A study in Finland found that the mortality from coronary heart disease restructured up to 49 percent in some segments of the population that restructured their diet. In hypertensive therapy, more than any other aspect of medicine, the role of dietary factors has entered into orthodox medical thinking.

Cholesterol-Lowering Drugs. Cholesterol-lowering drugs like Mevacor are associated with increased accidents, because of depletion of serotonin. So, while the drugs may lower your cholesterol, you pay a price in the brain. The objective is this: When heart disease is treated, be sure to build up the brain simultaneously, thus avoiding the deleterious effect of drugs on the nervous system. Previously, some cholesterol-lowering drugs have been linked to increased cancer and overall health problems. A lowered blood pressure is obtained when cholesterol is lowered, but this should be done naturally, or with careful attention to brain chemistry.

Lifestyle, Obesity, and Dietary Considerations

Numerous lifestyle factors have been identified in hypertension. A study in New York City, in which schoolchildren maintained ideal weight, decreased total and saturated fat, cholesterol, and sodium while increasing consumption of complex carbohydrates and fibers, showed improved blood pressure, plasma cholesterol, body mass index, and overall cardiovascular fitness. Even men with a genetic history of familial hypercholesterolemia can greatly reduce cardiovascular risks by eating a low-fat diet, doing regular aerobic exercise, strictly avoiding cigarettes, and monitoring blood pressure and blood cholesterol.

The sympathetic nervous system, which is activated by stress, isometrics, etc., plays an important role in creating hypertension. It has become increasingly clear that lifestyle changes can reduce excess catecholamine levels, which are potentially harmful chemicals that increase under stress. Nicotine from cigarette smoking causes small arterioles to constrict, blocks the useful effects of antihypertensive medicines, and is associated with malignant hypertension. Hypertensive rats reduced their own blood pressures simply through exercise.

A cold environment might correlate with higher blood pressure levels. Differences between winter and summer blood pressure in some people may be predictive of future hypertension. There is also some evidence that the roots of hypertension are found in early childhood and preventive attention should begin as early as adult blood pressures are achieved.

Obesity is the number-one lifestyle factor related to hypertension and probably overall health and longevity. Therefore, weight loss is an essential part of a high blood pressure treatment regimen. We do not, however, recommend appetite suppressants. One of these, phenylpropanolamine, can induce significant hypertension. Obesity is a major cardiovascular risk factor having a very complex socioeconomic, crosscultural interrelationship with various other risk factors. Hypertension has been shown to be directly proportional to obesity and glucose intolerance.

In a study with urban Bantus of Zaire, body weight and age were the major predictors of systolic and diastolic blood pressure. There is a wide variability of blood pressures among black people in Africa, suggesting that factors other than race play a role. A simple genetic explanation for the blood pressure differences between blacks and whites is inadequate and socioeconomic issues must be considered.

Diet and exercise such as walking, swimming and biking have beneficial effects on blood lipid levels. We always encourage our patients to exercise, if capable, usually after an EKG, 24-hour blood pressure monitor, and echocardiogram have been done, and, in some cases, after a stress thallium test. Exercise has been shown not to depress appetite but rather help to control it and is almost essential in a weight loss plan for hypertension. Simple exercise such as walking or swimming can add years to one's life. In a study where energy expenditure per week approached 3500 calories, illness also decreased significantly.

Seventh-Day Adventist lactovegetarians were compared with omnivorous Mormons (theoretically matching groups for effects of religiosity and abstention from alcohol, tobacco and caffeine). The lactovegetarians had lower blood pressure, even after adjusting for the effects of weight. Long-term adherence to a vegetarian diet was associated with less of a rise of blood pressure with age and a decreased prevalence of hypertension. Specific mechanisms and nutrients involved were not clarified.

Psychological, emotional and environmental factors also play a large role in cardiovascular disease, and this knowledge can be used to complement treatment regimens. Psychosocial and behavioral modification techniques are safe and somewhat effective in hypertension therapy. Feedback monitoring of blood pressure at intervals of several weeks was shown to be as effective as relaxation and biofeedback. Cranial electrical stimulation (CES), a stress and anxiety reduction technique, also may lower blood pressure.

An Australian study showed that after adjustment for different variables, the level of education was inversely related to blood pressure levels. Learning and education correlates with a healthier lifestyle and lower blood pressure.

Serum cholesterol correlates very closely to blood pressure levels and helps to identify the segment of the population in need of treatment. Elevated serum cholesterol (above 240 mg/dl) is the single, most important risk factor in coronary heart disease. In a study with more than 360,000 men, cardiovascular mortality rises steadily with increasing serum cholesterol levels (718 mg/dl). Aggressive dietary modifications are very useful to lower blood cholesterol levels which are linked to atherosclerotic vascular disease and coronary artery disease. Elevated serum and arterial cholesterol is a major entity in hypertension and cholesterol and can be reduced by dietary fibers such as bran and pectin. Dietary fibers contained in foods such as carrots and other vegetables lower body cholesterol levels by binding bile salts. Dietary fiber has an important moderating effect on serum cholesterol.

High-quality fresh and whole food sources of oils and animal products are important components of a healthful diet. Fatty acids (including polyunsaturated fats) and cholesterol are susceptible to degradation by oxidation and free radical reactions. Studies on animals show the resultant "oxy-cholesterols" have artery-clogging properties. Powders of egg and moldy cheeses (found in many fast foods) are especially harmful to the arteries.

Serum cholesterol and changes in serum cholesterol levels correlate to consumption of fats. However, serum cholesterol levels are not significantly related to dietary cholesterol in conjunction with a diet rich in polyunsaturated fats. A very high cholesterol intake by rural South African blacks, for example, caused no meaningful blood lipid fluctuations.

Furthermore, egg intake coupled with a diet low in other

saturated fats and high in polyunsaturated fats does not significantly raise blood cholesterol. Polyunsaturated fats can be used to lower total serum cholesterol and to raise HDL level, and thus can help to prevent atherosclerosis. Therefore, up to seven eggs per week are permitted for most hypertensive patients (unless they have an extremely elevated or refractory high cholesterol level).

Interestingly, animal studies suggest that sucrose (found in cane sugar and some fruits and vegetables) has the effect of raising blood pressure. Americans in particular consume large amounts of refined sugar. At high levels of carbohydrate consumption (50 to 80 percent) increased blood pressure is also noted. Some researchers believe that the dietary factors in hypertension may relate to the excess calories of saturated fat intake as well as high cholesterol and salt intake.

On the other hand, a diet rich in fruits, vegetables, whole grains and low-fat dairy items can protect against hypertension. An epidemiological study showed that one Chinese group with a history of hypertension had a high intake of added salt to their milk and tea, and consumed little starchy food, fresh fruits and vegetables. Consumption of proteins, animal fats, disaccharides, animal products, refined foods and high daily energy content of food were directly related to congestive heart disease (CHD), arteriosclerosis, myocardial infarction, and arteriosclerosis mortality, whereas consumption of vegetable fats, starch, cellulose, hemicellulose, pectin, vegetables, and fruit shared an inverse correlation.

Hypertensive patients may have impaired glucose tolerance, especially when treated with diuretics. Glucose tolerance tests in hypertensive patients are frequently abnormal. A high carbohydrate (sucrose) diet has been shown to induce sodium retention, and thus, through this retention of sodium, raise systolic blood pressure. A diet high in sucrose will raise blood pressure in animals significantly, possibly due to relative decrease in potassium intake. Glucose intolerance, obesity and blood pressure are tightly interrelated, so an imbalance in one will cause problems in the others.

Significant decreases in the consumption of calcium, potassium, vitamin A and vitamin C have been identified as nutritional factors that distinguish hypertensive from normotensive subjects. Calcium intake was the most consistent factor in hypertensive individuals. Previous reports showed a significant negative correlation between water hardness and mortality rates. A study comparing the twin Kansas cities in the United States showed the opposite to hold true: Hardwatered Kansas City, Kansas had more cardiovascular problems, including a tenfold higher serum cadmium level. Coffee has been shown to increase coronary heart disease risk by almost 250 percent. Smoking and hypertension are the two main risk factors for ischemic heart disease. Youngsters who smoke even less than one pack of cigarettes per day increase blood cholesterol and triglycerides.

Alcohol consumption also plays a role in hypertension. Moderate use of alcohol may lower blood pressure, but excessive use may elevate it. At moderate levels of one drink per day, alcohol has been shown in some cases to be protective against coronary artery disease. Alcohol in large doses may lead to rhythmic disturbances in the electrophysiology of the heart. Alcohol use may lead to depression in some individuals (it acts as a depressant), and increase carbohydrate consumption which will lead to hypertension.

In light of these findings, we recommend the following dietary guidelines to most of our hypertensive patients: low sodium, low saturated fat, and low refined carbohydrate intake, with high vegetable intake from the starch group and high salad and protein intake (particularly fish). Fresh cheeses are emphasized above aged cheeses. Simple sugars, alcohol, caffeine, nicotine and refined carbohydrates should be reduced drastically or eliminated.

Saturated Fat and Fish Oil. Numerous researchers have suggested that saturated fats can raise blood pressure, while others have suggested the potential blood pressure-lowering effect of fish oil. Polyunsaturated fats can be used to lower total serum cholesterol and to raise HDL level, and thus can help to prevent atherosclerosis. Dietary fat modifications, such as an increase in polyunsaturated-to-saturated fat ratio and an overall decrease in percentage of fat in the diet, lower blood pressure and have favorable effects on serum lipid levels. Greenland and Icelandic Eskimos, whose diets are rich in saturated fats, have a much lower incidence of coronary heart disease than controls because of high fish consumption. An inverse relationship was found with fish consumption and twenty-year mortality from coronary heart disease. Those who consumed 30 grams or more of fish per day had a 50-percent lower cardiac mortality rate than those who did not. Fish oils (omega-3 fatty acids) reduce high levels of plasma lipids, lipoproteins, and apolipoproteins in patients with high triglycerides. They also affect serum lipid levels in health humans. Eicosapentaenoic acid (EPA or fish oil) lowers abnormal blood lipid levels and decreases blood viscosity. Fish oil, like niacin, raises HDL and reduces risk from heart disease. Atherosclerosis formation is a very complex problem and may be related to an intracellular deficiency in essential fatty acids. Halberg suggested in 1983 that dietary lipid controls may be even more important than salt restriction in the control of hypertension.

Fish oils, especially the omega-3 fatty acids, have been shown to decrease risk of coronary heart disease. A diet high in fish or fish oil supplementation is recommended in patients with increased risk of coronary heart disease. In doses of up to 16.5 grams, fish oil has been shown to significantly lower blood pressure and cardiovascular risk factors.

Polyunsaturates and Hypertension. Both linoleic acid and dihomogammalinolenic acid (found in evening primrose oil) can be extremely useful in the treatment of hypertension. Fish oil, rich especially in omega-3 fatty acids, has been shown to lower blood pressure. Increasing consumption of monounsaturated fat is beneficial in lowering high blood pressure.

Again, dietary fat modification is an essential part of the treatment of hypertension; saturated fats have been definitively linked to high serum cholesterol. Dietary supplementation with linoleic acid, gamma-linoleic acid (GLA), or other polyunsaturated fatty acids is useful in controlling hypertension. These agents lower blood pressure and have both a diuretic effect (particularly linoleic acid and gamma-linolenic acid) and a prostaglandin-E2 inhibitory effect. A diet of fish which is high in EPA, such as mackerel, has been shown to lower high blood pressure, serum triglycerides and LDL cholesterol, and raise HDL. Linolenic acid, a polyunsaturate, is helpful in the treatment and prevention of hypertension, probably due to its conversion to prostaglandins and/or other vascular regulators. Linoleic and linolenic acids are both prostaglandin precursors and are useful in hypertension therapy.

Cis-linoleic acid is converted to gamma linoleic acid and eventually to prostaglandin E which is a vasodilator and inhibitor of platelet aggregation. In other words, it keeps the arteries open and lessens clogging. At least eight different studies showed that safflower oil, linoleic acid, cod liver oil, and eicosapentaenoic (EPA) acid all lowered blood pressure significantly.

Omega-3 fatty acids prevent elevated triglycerides induced by carbohydrates. Angina patients showed a lower ratio of EPA to AA (arachidonic acid). An olive oil-rich diet has been shown to decrease non-HDL cholesterol while leaving triglyceride levels constant. Eicosapentaenoic acid in the form of cod liver oil or mackerel is an excellent polyunsaturate and lowers cardiovascular risk factors.

Hence, all our patients were treated with EPA in the form of fish oils and omega-3, linoleic acid (safflower oil) or gamma-linolenic acid (primrose oil)—or all three. Dietary fatty acid intake is of particular importance in relation to blood pressure when weight reduction is occurring, as is the case with our patients.

Vitamin E. High levels of vitamin E are essential for preventing heart attacks and may be more important in preventing heart attacks than monitoring cholesterol. Unfortunately, polyunsaturates may lower vitamin E levels. So it is important to obtain ample amounts of vitamin E in a diet high in polysaturated oils. It is also notable that high levels of vitamin E, probably in the range of 1600 to 2000 units, may raise blood pressure slightly and that should be watched. In conclusion, vitamin E is important to the antioxidant reversal of both high blood pressure and heart disease.

Calcium. Numerous studies in the U.S. and elsewhere suggest that calcium may have an important role in hypertension. Hypertensive patients showed significant deficiencies in dietary calcium, potassium, vitamin A and vitamin C, with low calcium being the most consistent dietary risk factor for hypertension. Some reports show that oral calcium supplements (1 to 2 grams per day) lower blood pressure in some patients, particularly in young adults, possibly more so in women. Oral calcium carbonate administration also seems to have an effect on mild hypertensives. Calcium citrate is probably the best therapy.

In one study, calcium supplementation reduced blood pressure in young adults. Calcium supplementation of up to 1000 g has been shown to lower blood pressure in mild to moderate hypertension. Furthermore, surveys have shown a positive relationship between blood pressure and serum calcium levels. Acute elevation of circulating calcium levels during elevation of blood pressure, chronic hypercalcemia or hyperthyroidism, and vitamin D intoxication, are all associated with increased chronic hypertension. Calcium supplementation may lower elevated blood pressure by increasing sodium excretion. Three clinically paradoxical findings in the relationship of calcium and hypertension are as follows: calcium mediates vascular smooth muscle; calcium channel blockers lower blood pressure; and increased calcium intake can also relieve hypertension.

In contrast, several studies have shown that calcium can be a factor in *elevating* hypertension. Therefore, we use calcium sparingly except in the case of a woman suspected of having osteoporosis or in cases of normal plasma, ionized calcium or red blood cell calcium. Furthermore, vitamin D is also necessary in blood pressure control. So when we use calcium supplements, we use them with vitamin D.

Magnesium. Magnesium is well-known for its ability to lower blood pressure and has been used in the treatment of hypertension in pregnancy for decades. Magnesium, calcium, phosphorous, potassium, fiber, vegetable proteins, starch, vitamin C and vitamin D showed an inverse relationship with blood pressure with magnesium's correlation being the strongest, studies show.

Magnesium is a vasodilator and can at high levels cause low blood pressure. The use of various nutritional substances as pharmacological agents for hypertension has produced many success stories. Magnesium therapy has since been instituted for hypertension to combat a deficiency state often inflicted by diuretic usage. Magnesium deficiency may relate to high blood pressure by increasing microcirculatory changes or microcirculatory arteriosclerosis.

It has been suggested that magnesium supplements have a valuable effect on diabetic and hypertensive rats. Magnesium's use has been documented in cardiac situations, such as digitalis toxic arrhythmias due to magnesium depletion and myocardial infarctions due to decreases in potassium. Magnesium may be an important preventive in hypertensive patients prone to arrhythmia. Untreated hypertensives showed lower levels of intracellular free magnesium which strongly correlates to systolic and diastolic blood pressure. Hypertensive patients using diuretics had a magnesium level of 1.79 mg to 100 ml compared to normotensive patients with 1.92 mg to 100 ml, a significant difference. Magnesium is also low in the blood cells of cardiac patients in intensive care. Furthermore, we have shown in seven patients a significant decrease in red blood cell magnesium as compared to the mean of normotensive individuals. Type A personalities have been shown to lose red blood cell magnesium under stress and thus show a correlation to their tendency to develop hypertension and ischemic heart disease.

Magnesium deficiency has been shown to be sometimes related to dietary habits. Hence, many of our patients receive magnesium. In addition, many of our hypertensive patients who tend to have constipation find that it is relieved by magnesium.

Sulfur Amino Acids. Decreases in plasma taurine and methionine may be significant in patients with essential hypertension. Taurine may lower blood pressure. Furthermore, all sulfur amino acids—methionine, cysteine and taurine—lower heavy metals which are often factors in hypertension.

We have found a trend toward decreases in plasma cystine, probably due to B6 deficiency. Hence, most of our patients with hypertension receive supplemental sulfur amino acid treatment. Three grams of taurine daily could elevate blood taurine levels two to three times normal. We considered this an appropriate level to reach for hypertensives. Paradoxically, plasma taurine was elevated in our patients.

Sodium and Potassium. The role of dietary sodium in hypertension is long standing and well-known. According to the Tufts University *Diet and Nutrition Letter* in 1985, the average person consumes 10 to 12 g of sodium, which should be reduced to 2300 mg per day. This can be counterbalanced by increasing potassium intake, which may lower blood pressure. A higher ratio of potassium to sodium has been shown to lower moderately high blood pressure. Potassium therapy is useful in lowering blood pressure induced by diuretic-induced hypercalcemia. An inverse relationship between serum potassium and blood pressure has been shown. High potassium intake greatly reduced brain hemorrhages, infarctions and death rate in hypertensive rats. A high potassium intake may help to alleviate high blood pressure, the leading risk factor for smokers.

The hazards of high sodium intake go beyond hypertension and include gastric cancer. Dietary sodium affects urinary calcium and potassium excretion in men with regular blood pressure and differing calcium intakes. Researchers have suggested that stress and salt are cyclical, meaning increased salt intake produces stress and craving salt is a sign of stress. Dietary sodium and copper have long-term effects on elevating blood pressure in the Long-Evans research group of rats. Many researchers have shown that decreased sodium intake can decrease stress.

Some essential hypertensives have a low sodium-to-potassium and/or a high lithium-to-sodium counterpart. One study shows that hypertension in hypertensive rats is caused by a circulating hypertensive agent produced by the kidneys and adrenals whose secretion can be suppressed by volume or salt depletion. Hence, all of our patients are asked to restrict sodium as completely as possible and use salt substitutes. We suggest to all our patients that they use high potassium salt substitutes.

Trace Elements. Numerous studies have suggested that elevations in serum copper can raise blood pressure. Excess dietary copper can increase systolic blood pressure in rats. Elevations in serum copper and cadmium have been found in smokers, which may be the reason why they have elevated blood pressure. Contraceptive pill users have elevations in serum copper and elevations in arterial pressure. Patients who suffered from myocardial infarctions had decreased levels of zinc and iron but increased nickel levels, a 1984 study found. Hypertensive subjects who use diuretics have significantly higher serum copper levels. Increased serum copper has a role in primary or pulmonary hypertension. Zinc lowers serum copper and may actually lower blood pressure, and higher dietary zinc intake has been associated with lower blood pressure. Zinc is depleted by diuretics.

Increased red cell content of zinc in essential hypertension has been found by several researchers. Zinc is a well-known antagonist of heavy metals such as cadmium and lead, which even in chronic dosages have been found to elevate blood pressure. Hence, all our hypertensive patients receive zinc to lower copper, lead, cadmium and manganese. Studies have suggested that subacute elevations in cadmium and lead have a role in the elevation of blood pressure.

Blood lead levels, which are elevated in chronic alcoholism, have been correlated with increases in blood pressure. The correlation of blood lead to blood pressure is stronger for systolic than diastolic blood pressure. An overabundance of lead can lead to a form of hypertension with renal impairment. The lead content of the ventricles and aorta of myocardial infarction victims was consistently greater than for normal patients though not significant. Serum zinc levels were significantly lower for older hypertensive women and older men with high systolic readings. Elevations of lead and cadmium with decreases in zinc are a factor in many inner city patients with hypertension. Plasma zinc levels were significantly lower in patients having coronary heart disease risk factors. Furthermore, it has been shown that vitamin C in combination with zinc may be an even more effective way of reducing subacute levels of lead and cadmium. Hence, manganese levels are directly correlated to LDL and inversely correlated to HDL. We have had every patient follow a treatment plan which included zinc therapy. It is a consistent clinical observation to see rises in blood pressure with as little as 20 mg of manganese per day.

Vitamin B6. It has been established that vitamin B6 or pyridoxine deficiency has a role in hypertension. Vitamin B6 inhibits platelet aggregations through its metabolite, pyridoxal 5' phosphate. Pyridoxine deficiencies can elevate blood pressure. Vitamin B6 seems to relieve edema and swelling and thus has mild diuretic properties, therefore all our patients receive pyridoxine.

Niacin. Niacin, possibly because of its flush or vasodilating producing properties, can lower blood pressure as a vasodilator and can raise HDL fraction, which is frequently reduced in hypertensive patients. Niacin administration is a very effective agent against an increased level of LDL in patients with type II hyperlipoproteinemia. It also significantly raises HDL levels. Niacin has also been shown to reduce the average numbers of lesions per subject and block new atheroma formation. Niacin, when used alone or in conjunction with the drug colestipol, can effectively lower cholesterol and reduce triglyceride levels to 10, the normal physiological range. Niacin is used as an adjunct therapy in our treatment.

Selenium and Chromium. Serum selenium in patients with acute myocardial infarction was determined to be low before this condition occurred and not as a result. Chromium concentrations in aortas of patients dying from atherosclerotic disease are significantly lower as compared to a control group, where plasma chromium was found in patients with coronary artery and heart diseases. Both selenium and chromium may have a role in the nutritional control of hypertension, at least in the protection from myocardial infarction during a difficult dietary period.

Tryptophan. Tryptophan may have a role in hypertension, too. Studies have established that tryptophan in dosages of 3.5 g/day can lower blood pressure.

It is not, however, possible right now to use tryptophan for this purpose. After some serious health problems, including some deaths, resulting from a contaminated batch of tryptophan some years ago, the Food and Drug Administration has banned its use in the United States. At this point the problem with tryptophan seems to me to be a problem with the FDA. I don't think the literature supports the existence of serious side effects from tryptophan independent of contamination. It's impossible for me to believe that any scientist would think that tryptophan could present a serious health hazard, since it was regularly consumed by a large population without ill effects. All the other amino acids are used frequently with so few reported side effects that the idea of danger from tryptophan is absurd. I can only assume that the official opposition to tryptophan will not last much longer, and that it will soon be available by prescription. We do in fact have hydroxtryptophan available by prescription.

Other Nutrients. Vitamin C stabilizes vascular walls and helps metabolism of cholesterol into bile acids. When elderly patients receive 3 g of inositol, their total blood lipid and cholesterol levels decreased.

Garlic has been shown to be of great benefit in hypertension therapy, raising HDL and lowering both the total cholesterol and LDL. Garlic oil decreases platelet aggregation, serum cholesterol, and mean blood pressure, while it raises HDL and red blood cell arachidonic acid. Thus, garlic has been shown to be an antiatherosclerotic, antithrombotic, and an antihypertensive agent. Vitamin E lowers cholesterol and effects prostaglandin synthesis, yet vitamin E, by clinical observation, raises blood pressure.

One study has shown that nutritional and hormonal treatments can enhance the sodium potassium ATPase activity level and in turn helps to prevent or treat essential hypertension. Another study has shown that estrogen given to postmenopausal women reduces heart attack risk. Alcohol abuse, lead poisoning, birth control pills (estrogen), licorice (glycyrrhizinicals), diseases of the kidney, adrenal or pituitary glands, pregnancy and preeclampsia are some common causes of hypertension.

Numerous studies suggest the benefits of 24-hour blood pressure monitoring. This is an extremely important breakthrough in the management of hypertension.

Body composition testing can help predict and follow overall recovery from obesity and the natural approaches toward blood pressure.

It has been suggested that the borage oil supplement may be even better than the primrose oil supplement in lowering blood pressure.

Hypertension and nutrition research marches onward. Everyone with hypertension and/or a family history needs a dietary and nutritional regimen.

BIOCHEMICAL INDIVIDUALITY/GENETIC DIFFERENCES

It is very important for both the physician and hypertension patient to realize that every human being is genetically and biochemically distinct. Dietary or drug regimens have different effects on different patients. The influence of diet on blood lipid levels is not predictable for each individual due to different genetic traits. Sodium restriction is generally recommended in an antihypertensive diet, and, in most cases, this reduces blood pressure through volume effects. Sodium restriction is beneficial for the majority of hypertensives, but a recent epidemiologic study showed sodium restriction to be of no value in a small subgroup of the population at large. Furthermore, in a small group of patients, sodium *restriction* actually increases the activity of the angiotensin system and thus raises blood pressure. Some studies indicate that dietary sodium restrictions show differences in responses due to genetic differences in the renin-angiotensin-aldosterone system.

Dietary cholesterol, as found in eggs for example, usually does not significantly raise serum cholesterol in most patients if the patient is on a proper dietary regimen. Nevertheless, not all patients can consume large quantities of eggs without an increase in serum cholesterol. The dietary recommendations made in this book work exceptionally well in a vast majority of the hypertensive population, but some trial and error might be needed to tailor the program to your specific biochemical needs. Clinical judgment of which nutrient and diet to use can be refined by measuring plasma fatty acids, plasma amino acids, red-blood cell trace elements, hair analysis and vitamin levels. Following sed rates, cholesterol, apolipoproteins and fibrinogen levels are also useful. All of these tests can be done at your health care provider's office.

CASE HISTORIES

Removal of Multiple Drugs. G. F. is a 51-year-old male on multiple medications, weighing 265 pounds with a 25-year history of smoking two packs of cigarettes per day. He stopped smoking three years ago. He had BP of 150/100 and 140/100 with a pulse of 74. He was taking Aldomet, Klotrix, and Hydrochlorothiazide for ten years and Nitropatch nightly. He was put on a weight reducing, low-carbohydrate diet and started on a multivitamin, six per day; B6, 500 mg; magnesium orotate, 3 g; garlic, 1440 mg; taurine, 3 g; primrose oil (dihomogammalinoleic acid), 3 g; Max-EPA (eicosapentaenoic acid), 6 g; magnesium oxide, 1.5 g per day; and Klotrix, four per day or 40 mcg. Blocadren was reduced to two and Aldomet reduced to one.

After one month, his BP was 144/104 (increase in BP can occur with early reversal drugs), weight 248, and on 1/28 his BP was 120/88 and weight 249. Aldomet was stopped and Blocadren was maintained. On 2/11 his BP was 140/90, pulse 78, and weight 235. Blocadren was reduced to one pill, but he still used Nitropatch. On 3/11 BP was 140/94 and weight 226, and Blocadren was stopped. Taurine was reduced to 2 g and garlic to 960 mg. He was no longer on any medication except Nitropatch for BP. Klotrix was reduced to three tablets, and fish oil was switched to Mega-EPA, a more potent brand of EPA. On 4/10 his BP was 150/90, pulse 78, and weight 216. On 5/23 his BP was 130/70, pulse 80, and weight 214 pounds, and Nitropatch was stopped. Medication was reduced to four multivitamins; four garlic, 60 mg; taurine, 3 g; primrose oil, 2 g; fish oil, 6 g; and his antihypertensive formula was stopped. From 3/11 on he was taking two zinc pills per day, magnesium oxide 1000 mg (substituted for magnesium orotate), and niacin, 1 g per day. Safflower oil, 2 Tbsp. per day was also prescribed from 3/11 on, and vitamin C, 2 g per day from 4/10 on. Chromium, 200 mcg, one tablet/day, was taken from 5/22 on.

Hence, this patient, through the use of mega-nutrient therapy, was completely removed from drugs. His BP remains stable at 130/70. On 12/19 his cholesterol was 290 and triglycerides were 280. On 3/27 his triglycerides were 122 and cholesterol 223. He occasionally used vodka, coffee and tea. His sex drive was increased gradually throughout the treatment, and exercise (walking) gradually increased.

2. Removal of Beta-Blockers. A 42-year-old male, 5'10", weighing 179.5, was on Corgard for two years, drinking two cups of coffee a day, with a high sex drive and craving for salt. His BP was 150/90 on 5/16, and he was started on multivitamins, 500 mg vitamin B6, 200 mcg folic acid, 250 mcg vitamin B12, 3 g magnesium orotate, 3 g taurine, 1500 mg garlic, 3 g primrose oil, and six antihypertensive heart formula. On 5/30 his BP was very good at 128/82. He was off Corgard, with a pulse of 86 and weight 173.

3. Removal of Beta-Blockers. A 51-year-old female with a ten-year history of hypertension was presented to us for treatment. She weighed 150 pounds at 5'3", and was taking Lopressor 50 mg a.m. and p.m. She did not smoke or use alcohol or tea. On 5/23 her BP was 194/120, with a pulse of 116. She began taking multivitamins, two vitamin B6, 500 mg, 60 mg folic acid (for atrophic vaginitis), 3 g magnesium orotate, 2 g magnesium oxide, 3 g taurine, 1440 mg of garlic, 6 g Mega-EPA, six antihypertensive heart formula pills. She returned on 6/12 with BP 160/100, having gone three weeks without a migraine for the first time in years.

Her regimen was adjusted to 50 mg magnesium orotate, 3 g magnesium oxide, 2 g taurine, 600 mg calcium carbonate, 3 primrose oil, 100 mg niacin, 200 mcg chromium, 200 mcg selenium, and 50 mg Lopressor with instructions to go off 50 mg of Lopressor if there was improvement in two weeks. She returned drug-free, and her BP was 130/80. The rapid recovery of this patient was due to following a stricter diet of fish two times daily, meat two to three times per week, 3 Tbsp.

safflower oil daily, and frequent use of ginger, garlic and onions.

4. Removal of Diuretics. A 57-year-old male, 5'6", came to us for treatment in December with a BP of 160/100. He was taking Corgard, had a moderate sex drive, and did not use caffeine, did not exercise, and had a 30-year history of hypertension. He started on two Glucose Tolerance Factor (GTF) a.m. and p.m., 1 g vitamin C a.m. and p.m., Ziman (zinc 10 mg, manganese 2 mg) 10 drops, selenium 200 mcg a.m., molybdenum, Max-EPA 6 g/day, taurine 500 mg/day, magnesium orotate 2 g/day, and Corgard was reduced to 30 mg/day.

On 1/8 niacin was added (timed-release evening), and his weight had fallen to 154, with BP 120/75. On 2/5, Corgard was reduced to half a pill every other day, and he was advised to stop it in two weeks. Safflower oil 1 Tbsp. a.m. and p.m. was added, zinc 50 mg a.m. and p.m., dolomite (routine dose) one a.m. and p.m. and all medications remained stable. On 3/17 he was feeling light-headed and came in with a BP of 85/70 and a pulse of 90. Medication remained the same (he should have stopped Corgard 2/19), but safflower oil was stopped. He returned on 4/1 with BP 132/62, pulse 62, and weight 149. Initially his triglycerides were 256, cholesterol 190, and HDL fraction was 26 (high coronary risk). On 3/17 triglycerides were normal at 153, with cholesterol of 176 and an HDL fraction of 41 with all drugs removed.

5. Removal of Diuretics. A 62-year-old female, 5'3", with a 15-year history of hypertension came to us for treatment. She had been treated for 20 years with Hygroton 50 mg/day and Zyloprim (because of gout induced by Hygroton). Eighteen years ago she went through menopause and as a result had a diminished sex drive. Her BP was 160/100 and her weight was 204. Hygroton was stopped, and she was put on a Dyazide (instead of a diuretic) every other day. She was then permitted no fried or salted foods and was asked to follow a low-carbohydrate diet. She was started on a multivitamin one per day in July, chromium, 200 mcg a.m. and p.m., vitamin C, 2 g a.m. and p.m., vitamin B6, 500 mg in the a.m.; taurine, 1 g per day; primrose oil, 2 g a.m. and p.m.; zinc, 50 mg a.m. and p.m.; and safflower oil, 1 Tbsp. a.m. and p.m. The diuretic was finally stopped on 12/9, and her medication was changed to one multivitamin a.m. and p.m., vitamin B complex-50, one per night; GTF one 1 a.m. and p.m.; niacin 500 mg a.m. and p.m.; 500 mg vitamin B6, a.m.; vitamin C, ½ Tbsp. a.m. and p.m.; thyroid, 1 grain a.m. (per lab results); selenium, 200 mcg a.m.; kelp two a.m. and p.m.; Max-EPA, 1 g a.m. and p.m.; taurine, 500 mg a.m. and p.m.; zinc, 60 mg p.m. On 4/30 her BP was 130/70, and she was without the use of diuretics, and her vitamins were reduced gradually without elevation of blood pressure.

6. Fifteen-Year History of Hypertension.

A 53-year-old male, 5'11½", with a fifteen-year history of hypertension, taking one Maxzide a day, 300 mg Lopressor a day, 20 mg Minipress a day, and one Zyloprim, 300 mg a day for the treatment of gout came to us. He had a moderate sex drive, drank two cups of coffee a day, and had as many as three to seven drinks per week. His BP was initially 130/85, pulse 66, and weight 209 pounds. His triglycerides were 327, HDL 46 percent, and he had a high cholesterol of 255. He was started on one multivitamin a day, GTF 2 mcg a.m. and p.m., niacin 400 mg time-release a.m. and p.m., vitamin B6 500 mg a.m., vitamin C, calcium and magnesium powder 1 to 2 tsp. a.m. and p.m., magnesium orotate 500 mg a.m. and p.m., taurine 500 mg a.m. and p.m., methionine 500 mg a.m. and p.m., Mega-EPA (a more potent brand of EPA) 2 a.m. and p.m., and zinc gluconal a.m. and p.m.

Maxzide was changed to every other day and he was instructed to stop it if light-headedness developed. He was put on a carbohydrate-deprivation diet and a protein and vegetable diet with no bread or fruit. On 5/6 he returned with BP of 118/78, pulse 60, and weight 196 pounds. During that period Lopressor had been reduced to 100 mg a.m. and p.m. by phone conversation, Minipress was 5 mg a.m. and p.m., and Maxzide was stopped based on BPs done at home on his machine. On 5/6, vitamin C was reduced due to diarrhea, but the other supplements were virtually the same, but generally increased GTF up to 200 mg, two tabs, a.m. and p.m., multivitamin a.m. and p.m., niacin increased to three times a day, vitamin B6 500 mg a.m., selenium 200 mcg, methionine 500 mg a.m. and p.m., taurine 1 gram a.m. and p.m., magnesium orotate (reduced because of diarrhea), Mega-EPA 3 g a.m. and p.m., primrose oil a.m. and p.m., and zinc 15 mg a.m., 30 mg p.m.

On 5/27 the patient returned with BP of 120/80, weight 188, triglycerides now normal at 97, cholesterol reduced to 238, and HDL increased 51 percent. Patient had now gradually reduced Minipress to 5 mg/day and Lopressor 100 mg every other day, magnesium oxide was stopped due to diarrhea, zinc gluconate 15 mg a.m., 30 mg p.m., lithium one p.m., mega EPA 3 g a.m. and p.m., taurine 1 g a.m. and p.m., tryptophane 500 mg a.m. and p.m., methionine 100 mg a.m. and p.m., niacin reduced to two per day, GTF twice a day, and a multivitamin doubled a.m. and p.m.

On 6/25 the patient returned with a weight of 184, BP 110/80, having been on Lopressor 100 mg every other day, and pulse 75. He was now put on Lopressor (50 mg/day). On 7/15 the patient was drug-free and had BP of 120/80 consistently over multiple readings.

7. Heart Formula for Blood Pressure Lowering. A 53-year-old male with a fifteen-year history of poorly controlled hypertension came to us being treated with diuretics, Minipress, Lopressor, and Zyloprim. He was taken off all drugs with the simple application of weight loss and the mega-nutrient therapy, ten pills a day of antihypertensive heart formula.

8. Getting Off Diuretics. A 65-year-old female, 5'6", with a long history of hypertension, who had been treated with diuretics, with BP 170/110, pulse 102, weight 170, triglycerides 70, cholesterol 234, HDL 65, was presented to us and was placed on a low-carbohydrate diet and supplement regimen. This included: GTF one a.m. and p.m., niacin timed-release 2 g a.m., 1 g p.m., vitamin B6 500 mg a.m., vitamine # 400 mg a.m. and p.m., vitamin A 24,000 IU a.m., selenium 200 mcg a.m., Max-EPA 3 g a.m., 2 g at noon, 3 g p.m., tyrosine 2 g a.m., methionine 1 g a.m., dolomite two at bedtime, and Ziman fortified one a.m. and p.m.

The patient returned on 1/21 with BP 152/90, with a weight of 164, and was put on Max-EPA and primrose oil 1 gram a.m. and p.m., vitamin C 2½ g a.m. and p.m., safflower oil 1 tsp. a.m. and p.m. She then returned on 4/15 with BP 110/85 without medication, pulse 78, and weight of 162. Her BP is well-controlled on this regimen and her caffeine consumption has been stopped.

9. Formerly Treated with Dyazide and Lopressor. A 45-year-old female, 5'5", treated with Dyazide and Lopressor, had a BP of 130/80, weight 105, triglycerides 115, and cholesterol 178. She started with multivitamins once a day, GTF 200 mcg once in the a.m., niacin 400 mg timed-release a.m. and p.m., vitamin B6 500 mg a.m., methionine 500 mg a.m. and p.m., tryptophan 1 gram before sleep, taurine 500 mg a.m., primrose oil 1½ g a.m. and p.m., Max-EPA 1 g a.m. and p.m., bone meal (a calcium supplement) 1 a.m. and p.m., and zinc 15 mg a.m. and p.m. Dyazide was reduced to two a day and one the next, and Lopressor was stopped. On 8/1 she was taking Lopressor every other day as well as Dyazide, with essentially the same regimen of vitamins. By 11/12 her BP was 110/80, pulse 80, and weight 109. She was off all BP medication.

In sum, this patient highlights the growing effect of nutrients over time, with very little change in her diet, by the way, except for the reduction of fried foods, caffeine and white flour.

10. Taken Off Diuretics. A 59-year-old man, 5'8", with a weight of 227, on HydroDiuril for ten years, was presented to us with BP 120/80, pulse 60, trigylcerides 298, and cholesterol 173. He was started on GTF 200 mg 1 a.m. and p.m., vitamin C 500 mg a.m. and p.m., vitamin B6 500 mg a.m., beta-carotene

50 mg/day, selenium 200 mcg a.m., Max-EPA 2 a.m. and p.m., cysteine 100 mg a.m. and p.m., dolomite 2 a.m. and p.m., and Ziman fortified 1 a.m. and p.m. He was put on a high vegetable, low fruit, low-carbohydrate diet, and Maxzide was changed to one tablet every other day. He was put on safflower oil 2 tsp. a.m. and p.m. and taken off of caffeine beverages. Due to light-headedness, the patient had to stop Maxzide shortly thereafter.

On 12/18 his BP was 120/90 without a diuretic, and his weight was up to 238. Vitamins were kept the same except for Max-EPA which was increased to 4 g a.m. and p.m., and taurine was started at 500 mg a.m. and p.m. On 3/17 his triglycerides were normal at 153, with cholesterol of 176, and the HDL fraction was improved. By 5/14 his BP was 120/80, and his pulse was 60 without medication. His weight is 227, and he still continues to do well without medication, diuretic-free, and has reduced his vitamins by one-half.

11. Ten-Year History of Hypertension. A 56-year-old female, 5'10", with a ten-year history of hypertension came to us. She drank one to two cups of coffee a day, and presented to us with a BP of 160/90, pulse 80, weight 185, triglycerides 154, and cholesterol 233, while taking one Dyazide daily. She was started on one multivitamin tablet a day, GTF one a.m. and p.m., niacin 400 mg time-release, vitamin B6 500 mg a.m., taurine 500 mg a.m. and p.m., MegaEPA 1 gram a.m. and p.m., magnesium oxide 1 a.m. and p.m., and primrose oil 1 g a.m. and p.m.

She presented on 5/20 with a BP of 140/84, after having stopped diuretics, with a weight of 181 pounds. She had not even begun the magnesium or niacin. Later, she began these treatments and her BP was 120/80 and is well-controlled.

12. On Diuretics for Twenty Years. An 80-year-old female, 4'11", on diuretics for 20 years, drinking four cups of coffee daily, had a BP of 200/98, pulse 88, and weight 114¾. She was started on multivitamins, 500 mg vitamin B6, 2 g calcium penthienate, one zinc, one manganese, 3 g magnesium orotate, 1500 mg calcium orotate, 3 g taurine, 3 tabs of tyrosine and dl-phenylalanine. On 1/23 her BP was 180/90, pulse 78, and she was removed from diuretics.

Supplementation was changed to four multivitamins/day, 1 g calcium, 15 mg zinc 2/day, manganese was stopped, 2 g primrose oil was added, 3 g vitamin C and 2000 mg fish oil (EPA). On 2/20 her BP was 174/80, pulse 76, and weight was stable at 113½. Taurine was reduced to 2 g, primrose oil increased to 3½ g, vitamin C increased to 5 g, and fish oil to 3 g. On 3/21 her BP was 150/90, pulse 76, and weight 116. One Tbsp. safflower oil was added with 1 g magnesium. On 4/18 her BP was 150/80, pulse 76, and weight 114.

CONCLUSION

In summary, it appears that meganutrient therapy can replace much drug treatment, although there may be some difficulty in the age group of 75 and older due to a more advanced stage of the disease and individuals who present on two or more drugs. Catching the disease early and treating with the orthomolecular approach is the best answer. Treating hypertension can be an art and requires thyroid function tests, 24-hour free cortisol renal scan, intravenous pyelogram (IVP), 24-hour urine steroids, and plasma renin for the patients that do not respond to either drug or nutrient regimens. At this point we have had an extremely high success rate using mega-nutrients which have emphasized large dosages of magnesium (particularly in oxide form), large dosages of eicosapentaenoic acid (EPA) (up to 7 g), large dosages of primrose oil 2 to 3 g, safflower oil, vitamin B6 500 mg, taurine up to 3 g, methionine up to 1 g, niacin up to 2 g, zinc up to 60 mg, and garlic up to 1500 mg.

Although the number of nutrients replacing drugs can be an enormous amount, we have not seen significant side effects other than diarrhea from vitamin C and/or magnesium. We have seen virtually no side effects from these nutrients, and patients claim to feel better, do better, feel good about being drug-free, and have far less side effects than any other regimen so far reported. We usually suggest that all hypertension patients have an initial complete chemical screen, triglycerides, cholesterol, thyroid, as well as RBC magnesium, trace elements (selenium, chromium, zinc, lead, cadmium), plus amino acids and IgE allergy screen. Orthomolecular treatment of hypertension through diet and nutrients has arrived as a documented and successful approach.

BASELINE THERAPY FOR A TYPICAL HYPERTENSIVE

B6	200 mg
selenium	200 mg
primrose oil	1 gram a.m. & p.m.
GTF	200 mcg a.m.
fish oil	2 grams a.m. & p.m.
magnesium oxide	500 mg a.m. & p.m.
zinc	15 mg a.m. & p.m.
taurine	500 mg a.m. & p.m.
cysteine	500 mg a.m. & p.m.
garlic	Dr. Braverman's Heart Formula 3 pills in a.m. & p.m.
niacin	400 mg a.m. & p.m.
tryptophan	1 gram at bedtime
vitamin C	500 mg a.m. & p.m.
CoQ10	60–90 mg daily
potassium	10–25 mg

PATH (Products for Achieving Total Health)

Heart Formula, one to fifteen pills daily with other vitamins and medications as directed by physician. This supplement has been the most useful for treating hypertension.

Each tablet contains:

Garlic powder (odorless)	200 mg	Chromium (chloride)	26.7 mcg
Taurine	200 mg	Niacinamide	50 mg
Magnesium (oxide)	50 mg	Vitamin C	40 mg
Potassium (chloride)	6.7 mg	Molybdenum (chelate)	40 mcg
Selenium (sodium sel.)	20 mcg	Vitamin B6	50 mg
Zinc (chelate)	4 mg	Beta-carotene	1222 IU

DIET

- 2 Tbsp. safflower oil
- fish daily; poultry cooked without skin—often
- no food additives, sugar, refined foods, caffeine, or alcohol
- red meat once a week
- high vegetables (nonstarchy type)
- high salad
- 1 slice whole-wheat bread (now frequently not allowed until any needed weight loss is accomplished)
- ½ fruit

TABLE 1
RBC Magnesium in Hypertension

Patient Groups		
	Control	Hypertension Beta-Blockers
RBC g	n = 50	n = 7
	4.4 ± 0.22mg/L	3.79 ± 1.57
(RBC mg $p < 0.00$)		

TABLE 2
Plasma Sulfur Amino Acids in Hypertension

	Control	Hypertension
Cystine	n = 16 2.3 ± 1.5	n = 7 2.97 ± 1.57
Taurine	n = 16 5 ± 1.3	n = 7 6.86 ± 2.34
Methionine	n = 16 3 ± 0.9	n = 7 2.71 ± 0.76
(Taurine p < 0.03)		

Chapter 6

More Proof of the Program:
Ten Case Histories

The proof of any antihypertension and heart disease program is in the number of sufferers who are returned to a normal daily life with their high blood pressure and heart disease under control or reversed.

A top-notch program does more: It prevents the disorder from recurring. The Braverman Ten-Step Program will do both for you if you give it your all. Even if you follow the program with halfhearted attention, you'll be rewarded.

CASE 1

J. K. was a 62-year-old man with a ten-year history of hypertension with a cholesterol of 264, triglycerides of 161, HDL of 59. He was taking Normodyne, 50 mg Dyazide and Lopid. He was taken off all three drugs in one week. Because his initial presentation was a blood pressure of 140/90, and he was 136 pounds at 5'3", he was put on Plan A, a low-carbohydrate, high-protein diet. He returned about fifteen days later and his weight had fallen from 136 to 131, his cholesterol fell from 264 to 131, triglycerides went from 161 to 100, HDL went up to 64, his blood pressure was 120/80. All this was done over a two-week period when he was taking 8 primrose oil pills, 6 Mega-ML 1000 fish oil pills, 2 tsp. of liquid fish oil, 6 of my Hypertension Formula #1, 1 of Formula

#4, and 200 mg of a niacin garlic formula (Niagar). Initially, in the first week, he stopped Dyazide, went to half dose of Normodyne, and in the second week he discontinued it. He was then continued on this program which also included 3 Tbsp. of safflower oil. Then he returned the following week with blood pressure of 110/80. Gradually, his vitamins were reduced and he was put on Plan B and is still doing fantastically well, drug-free. His energy level and sex drive have increased enormously.

CASE 2

A 54-year-old man with a diagnosis of hypertension and renal insufficiency was placed on 6 capsules of fish oil, 8 capsules of primrose oil, 6 capsules of my Formula #1, 1 capsule of my Formula #4, 2 Niagar formula, 1 antioxidant capsule, and 1 N-acetyl-cysteine (500 mg). He was initially on Lopressor 50 mg and Hydrodiuril.

Within two weeks he tapered off them and his blood pressure, nevertheless, fell from 140/90 to 140/85. He is 6'2", 175 pounds. His initial cholesterol was 176 and HDL was 44. Two-and-a-half months later, his cholesterol had fallen to 130 and his blood pressure was normal at 130/82 on average and he was completely drug-free. Initial elevations in creatinine of 1.7 fell to 1.3 and he is still doing fine a year later, drug-free on basically the same regimen. His energy level and sex drive increased enormously.

CASE 3

A 55-year-old female with a five-year history of hypertension was taking the diuretic Lozol. Cholesterol was 250, triglycerides 639, her weight was 159 pounds at 5'2.5" and she ran a constant blood pressure of 176/100. She was put on 3 Tbsp. of fish oil liquid (because she preferred liquid to large capsules), 8 evening primrose oil, 8 of my Hypertension Formula

#1, 2 grams of niacin, as well as two Tbsp. of safflower oil and Magnesium Formula #4.

In one week her triglycerides fell from 639 to 166. In a period of one month her cholesterol fell from 250 to 225; her HDL level remained stable at about 32; weight fell from 159 to 148, and she discontinued her diuretic and had a blood pressure of 140/78. She continues to do extremely well with excellent control of her blood pressure and continued lowering of her cholesterol as she continues to lose weight on Plan A. When she reaches her ideal weight, she will be switched to Plan B. Her energy, happiness and sense of well-being have increased dramatically.

CASE 4

A 49-year-old female with a two-year history of borderline hypertension presented 5'3", 173 pounds, blood pressure consistently around 160/100, cholesterol 204, triglycerides were good at 75, and HDL 83. She was placed immediately on Plan A, as well as put on 3 fish oil capsules, 6 Evening Primrose oil capsules, 2 Formula #1, 2 of my Calcium Formula #3, 1 of my Magnesium Formula #4, my Antioxidant Formula, as well as 1500 mg of Niagar formula, Amino Stim (an amino acid combination for energy), and tryptophan complex for sleep.

In a period of five weeks she lost six pounds, and her blood pressure fell to 110/79, where it's remained over many months. She continued to lose weight. Three months later, she weighed 147 and had lost twenty pounds. Her blood pressure was 110/68. Her blood pressure is still monitored monthly, reading approximately 110/70 consistently. She continues on Plan A until she will be switched to Plan B (once she reaches normal weight) and will have a reduction in her pills. At this time, her energy level, sense of well-being and mood are at their best in her life.

CASE 5

This case pertains to a 55-year-old male with a history of a heart attack, cholesterol of 234, resistant to dietary treatment, triglycerides 289, HDL 30, 6'2", 172 pounds with a mild isolated systolic blood pressure of 140/80. He was placed on 2 Tbsp. of fish oil, 6 fish oil capsules, 8 evening primrose oil, 2 of my multivitamin, 4 of Hypertension Formula #1 and 3 grams of niacin. He is also taking Cardizem from which he has since been weaned.

In three weeks his cholesterol fell from 234 to 130, triglycerides fell from 289 to 123, HDL went up to 33, and his blood pressure normalized to 120/70. Six weeks later he had a cholesterol level of 114!—with an HDL of 47, and a pulse of 52 which had fallen from 68. With a reduction in supplements, his pulse and blood pressure returned to normal levels. His weight has fallen from 172 to 163, his blood pressure is 98/60, and he has been switched to Plan B. This has resulted in a significant reduction of his vitamins, and he was told to go off of Cardizem. His energy and sense of well-being have greatly improved.

CASE 6

This case resulted in the removal of two strong drugs with lowering of blood pressure. A 64-year-old female with a history of hypertension for thirteen years, as well as diabetes and depression, was treated with 150 mg Normodyne (a beta-blocker) daily and 10 mg Vasotec (angiotensin-2 enzyme inhibitor) daily. Initially, her blood pressure was 170/90.

I started her on the basic regimen of 2 capsules of magnesium, 4 capsules of taurine, 4 capsules of garlic, and 6 capsules of evening primrose oil. Both drugs were tapered off and her blood pressure temporarily increased one month later to 190/98.

To counteract this rise, we added 6 grams of fish oil, 1 g of magnesium, 400 mg niacin (time-release), plus 1 Tbsp. of safflower oil daily. We increased her garlic to six Heart Formula pills.

Seven days later, her blood pressure had fallen to 150/82, and three weeks later, it fell again to 140/80, where it has remained while on the current vitamin program and my Plan B diet, free of Normodyne and Vasotec.

CASE 7

In this case, two dangerous drugs were discontinued. It concerns a 68-year-old man, 6'1", 177 pounds, with a blood pressure of 120/80 and a pulse of 84. He had a five-year history of hypertension and was being treated with 250 mg Aldomet twice daily, and one Hydrochlorothiazide (a diuretic).

His initial program consisted of 500 mg B6, 2 g taurine (an amino acid), 4 capsules garlic, 6 capsules evening primrose oil, 6 capsules fish oil, 400 mg niacin, and 4 capsules of methionine (an amino acid). This diuretic was immediately discontinued and the Aldomet was discontinued a month later. Sixty days later, the patient had a regular BP of 130/80 without either drug.

Eight months later, with his blood pressure normalized, he had an HDL cholesterol reading that increased from 36 to 52, and triglycerides (TG) that went from 195 to 90. His good cholesterol (HDL) stayed essentially the same. Despite discontinuing two dangerous drugs, he had a complete reversal of his poor cardiovascular profile. He was then placed on the Plan B diet and five-step nutrient program (see pages 30, 56).

CASE 8

This case illustrates the healing of high blood pressure, reduction of high cholesterol and other heart risk factors without drugs. A 62-year-old female, with an eight-year history of hypertension, was being treated with 40 mg Lasix (a diuretic) per day, and 40 mg Visken (a beta-blocker) per day.

Her blood pressure was 180/100. She was started on 5

capsules garlic oil, 6 capsules evening primrose oil, 6 capsules fish oil, 1 g magnesium, 30 mg zinc, 500 mg B6, and a multivitamin.

Within thirty days her pressure read 130/80. Immediately her Lasix was stopped, and within another thirty days her BP stayed in the good category of 130/80. But when her Visken was stopped, her BP went up to 140/90. (Increases in blood pressure can occur in the early stages of drug reversal.)

She was then advised to take 8 g of fish oil and 4½ g of evening primrose oil. Her BP fell to the safe range of 130/80, where it remains today. Furthermore, her depression has lifted.

CASE 9

The elimination of multiple drugs was experienced by G. F., a 51-year-old male on multiple medications, weighing 265 pounds, with a 25-year history of two packs of cigarettes per day, who had stopped smoking three years ago.

His blood pressure read 150/100 with a pulse of 74. He had taken Aldomet, Klotrix, Blocadren and Hydrochlorothiazide for ten years. He was put on my weight-reducing, low-carbohydrate diet (Plan A) and started on a multivitamin, B6 500 mg, magnesium orotate 3 g, garlic 1440 mg, taurine 3 g, evening primrose oil 3 g, Super-EPA (eicosapentaenoic acid) 6 g, and magnesium oxide 1.5 g per day. His Klotrix was reduced to four per day. The diuretic was stopped and Aldomet reduced to one.

After 30 days, his BP was 144/104, weight 248. Shortly thereafter, his pressure had fallen to 120/88 and his weight 239. Aldomet was stopped and Blocadren was maintained. Thirty days later, his BP was 140/90, pulse 78, weight 235. Blocadren was reduced to one pill, but Nitropatch maintained. A month later, BP was 140/94 and weight had fallen to 226. Blocadren was stopped. Taurine was reduced to 2 g and garlic 900 mg. He was no longer on any medication except Nitropatch for BP. Klotrix (a potassium supplement) was reduced to three tablets, fish oil was switched to Mega-EPA (a more potent brand of EPA) and in thirty days his BP was 150/90, pulse 78, and weight 216 pounds. An additional thirty days later, BP was 130/70, pulse 80, and weight 214 pounds. The Nitropatch was stopped. Nutrients were reduced to 4 multivitamins, 600 mg of garlic, taurine 3 g, evening primrose oil 2 g, fish oil 6 g, and his antihypertensive formula was stopped. He was taking two zinc pills per day, magnesium oxide 1000 mg (substituted for magnesium orotate), and niacin 1 g per day. Two tablespoons per day of safflower oil was also prescribed and vitamin C, 2 g per day, plus chromium 200 mcg, 1 tablet per day.

In summary, this patient, through the use of mega-nutrient therapy, was completely removed from drugs. In three months, his BP remained stable at 130/70. Cholesterol 290 and triglycerides of 280 fell to 223 and 122, respectively, even though he occasionally uses vodka, coffee and tea. His sex drive has increased gradually throughout the treatment and exercise (walking) has gradually increased.

CASE 10

In this case, four types of drugs were eliminated and a return of the sex drive was experienced. A 49-year-old man, with a 20-year history of hypertension and a ten-year history of elevated triglycerides, came to me for help. He was on Lorelco (an antilipid drug) 250 mg three times a day, Lopressor (beta-blocker) 50 mg twice a day, and Apresoline (vasodilator) 100 mg three times a day, Hydrochlorothiazide (diuretic) 50 mg daily, and Anturane 200 mg twice daily. His sex drive was greatly diminished.

Initially he had a blood pressure of 150/95, while on the medicine. He was asymptomatic at this time. We immediately stopped his Lorelco because we knew that we could substitute fish oil for the Lorelco-type drugs. We also stopped the

Anturane, which was protecting him from gout (caused by his diuretic).

We put him on 8 capsules fish oil, 3 grams evening primrose oil, 1 g magnesium, 1 g carnitine (an amino acid), 500 mg vitamin B6, and some multivitamins.

Despite putting him on the low-carbohydrate diet, this 5'9½", 164-pound man had lost only two pounds when he returned eleven days later with a BP of 130/90.

We added 2 g taurine, 1 g garlic, 30 mg zinc, and 400 mg timed-released niacin to his program. We reduced Lopressor to 25 mg twice a day. In one month, he returned with a BP of 170/88. We put him on a stricter low-carbohydrate diet, discontinued Lopressor, and eventually tapered off Apresoline dose, substituting 1 pill of Vasotec (Vasotec has fewer side effects).

He returned six weeks later with BP readings between 120-140/70-80. We had previously added nutrients such as GTF and selenium and inositol. Blood pressure was well under control. He was off Lopressor and Apresoline and was just using Vasotec. Initially, he had an HDL of 41, triglycerides of 394, and a normal cholesterol of 205. In two months on diet Plan B, his HDL had jumped to 55, his triglycerides had fallen from 394 to 225, and his cholesterol remained essentially the same. Importantly, this patient's sex drive is now normal. In addition, there was tremendous improvement in his HDL fraction and a reduction in his triglycerides. In summary, without lipid-lowering drugs, his treatment was a complete success. His one-pill dosage of Vasotec does not produce any symptoms. Once a high-risk patient for heart disease and stroke, he is now becoming a low-risk patient.

Chapter 7

Six Commonly Asked Questions About the Braverman Plan

How Important Is Pulse?

Unnatural lows or highs in blood pressure are associated with a rapid pulse. Hence, another index of how dangerous your hypertension is, especially in the diastolic range of 90-95 or systolic 140-160, is pulse. Rapid pulse (greater than 80) can indicate hypertension or heart disease that needs further treatment.

Where Does the Hypertension and Heart Disease Danger Begin?

Stroke, heart attack, and other cardiovascular events such as aneurysm become greater at an increasing rate as systolic pressure rises. A systolic blood pressure of 100-110 is at the lowest and best. A diastolic blood pressure increases from 70-90, cardiovascular events increase. High risk begins with a diastolic over 95. All blood pressure must be checked first at basal level. As diastolic of 85 is high, while stress pressures (doctor's office anxiety) of 90 are high. Systolic pressure is the second consideration in risk prevention. The level of systolic pressure is also important in assessing arterial pressure's influence on cardiovascular morbidity. Males with normal diastolic pressures (<82 mmHg) but elevated systolic pressures (>158 mmhg) have a 2.5-fold increase in cardiovascular mortality rates when compared with individuals with normal systolic pressure (<130 mmHg; perhaps even less than 120 mmHg). Hence, nutrient and diet therapy is essential for hypertension.

What Factors Indicate a Bad Prognosis in Hypertension?

Factors that contribute to a bad prognosis in hypertension are: black race, youth (the younger you get it, the less likely the cure), male, persistent diastolic pressure >115, smoking, diabetes mellitus, hypercholesterolemia, obesity, and evidence of end-stage organ damage. Cardiac factors can include: cardiac enlargement, ECG changes of ischemic or left ventricular strain, myocardial infarction and congestive heart failure. Eye factors can include: retinal exudates, hemorrhages, retinopathy, and papilledema. Renal factors are basically impaired renal function. Nervous system factors include cerebrovascular accidents.

Does Very Mild Hypertension Need Treatment?

All hypertension reduces lifespan and quality of life. Mild hypertension treated through diet and nutrition has never needed drug treatment in my five years of experience. Moderate hypertension rarely if ever needs a drug because of the great effects of diet and nutrients. The blood pressure monitor defines patients who have borderline blood pressure or who just have anxiety-induced high blood pressure.

How Important Is Restricting Salt?

One of the most important findings in hypertension is that a low-salt diet is helpful. Generally speaking, because so many foods contain salt, there is no reason to use salt on food.

There is a new salt substitute being developed, ornithyl-taurine. These two amino acid peptides taste like salt. Furthermore, several different potassium-magnesium salt mixtures are available which are perfectly good tasting. There are also many well-known potassium-chloride salt substitutes that are now on the market. It is well known that salt increases blood volume and raises blood pressure.

Another potential way to reduce the craving for salt may be the use of supplemental magnesium or nickel. It has been shown that animals that are fed nickel have reduced salt appetite. Whether this has a bearing on humans is unclear at present. Possibly tyrosine may also reduce salt craving.

The brain controls the appetite for fats and salts. Brain chemical control of appetite for fats and salt has now been established. In the case of fat, it is a protein called galanin. We believe it can be reduced by certain amino acids, i.e., tyrosine, phenylalanine and methionine. The same is true concerning salt appetite—which seems to be regulated by serotonin metabolism. Salt restriction actually stimulates the serotonergic system in man. There is also an increase in noradrenaline excretion. It is thought that if you stimulate the serotonergic system with Prozac, melatonin or tryptophan, salt appetite may be reduced. But this is unclear at this time. We think and believe that salt appetite is increased by low levels of serotonin or adrenergic neurotransmitters and therefore the key amino acids, tyrosine, phenylalanine, methionine and tryptophan reduce salt appetite for some people who need to reduce their salt intake, particularly hypertensive patients and heart failure patients. Building up brain chemistry is an alternative route to strengthen the possibility of reduced heart disease. Thyroid hormone also can reduce salt appetite if it is slightly low. Levels of TSH that are above three may be considered hypothyroid. A strict interpretation of hypothyroidism may result in improvement. Anything that reduces anxiety, such as a CES device, may reduce salt appetite.

A few of the many risk factors for hypertension are as follows: drugs (alcohol, birth control pills), toxins (all heavy metals), metabolism disorders (any endocrine problem, e.g., hypothyroidism, Cushing's disease), male climacteric or female menopause (lack of sex hormones results in a rising cholesterol because all sex hormones are made from cholesterol. Without utilizing the cholesterol to synthesize sex hormones, naturally cholesterol builds up), heart disease (failure, arrhythmia), tumors (pheochromocytoma tumor, any primary tumor), and kidney disorders (artery stenosis, failure, glomerulonephritis). Many of these are underlying causes of hypertension. For decreased sexual function, natural testosterone and estrogen will actually help your blood pressure and heart. It is a shame not to take advantage of the natural hormone therapies. DHEA is also underrated with respect to how much it can improve sexual function, according to new studies.

Why Do Drugs for Hypertension Kill Your Sex Drive?

High blood pressure drugs often cause depression, worsening circulation, atherosclerosis, nutrient depletion of potassium and magnesium, depression neurologic response, and a decreasing sensitivity of heart and penis to excitation. There is a similar effect of decreased sexual drive in women. If you use a drug, beta-blocker or diuretic, you can almost count on a loss of sex drive and performance with prolonged use. My vitamin regimen is a tremendous success because it transforms bad cardiovascular risk profiles and provides valuable nutrients. Triglycerides, LDL, blood sugar, and cholesterol go down magnesium potassium, HDL and sexual appetite rise.

Chapter 8

Understanding the Ups and Downs of Blood Pressure

There is no single act you can do that will change your life as dramatically as taking control of your hypertension—and getting control of your life once more—and doing it without drugs.

But to understand what to do, first you must understand how normal blood pressure works, and how high blood pressure does its damage.

Blood pressure is the pressure of the blood in the body's arterial system—which carries oxygen-rich blood away from the heart and into the tissues, arterioles, and capillaries. After this, the blood enters the veins which transport blood back to the heart and lungs. The contractions and expansions of the heart as blood is pushed into the arterial system and let out to flow from the veins to the heart is interpreted by your doctor as *blood pressure,* and reported as a fraction.

How Blood Pressure Is Determined

A sphygmomanometer is the instrument used to measure blood pressure. The cuff is wrapped around your arm and tightened by means of a pump that inflates the cuff and cuts off most of the circulation in the arm. A valve is then released, allowing air to seep out and the cuff to loosen.

A stethoscope is placed over the artery located in the crook of the elbow. The pressure on the meter is read when enough air pressure has been released so the pulsing of blood can be heard through the stethoscope (this is systolic, the high number). The lower number is read when one stops hearing the pulse (this is diastolic, the lower number). Systolic pressure is the pressure of the blood against artery walls when blood is squirted out of the pumping heart. Diastolic pressure is the force of blood against arterial walls when the heart is at rest.

Adult blood pressure below 140/90 is in the normal range. 140/90 to 160/110 is mild to moderate elevation. Pressure over 160/110 is considered severe and beyond that "critical." But blood pressure has a lot of ups and downs. It can change in a matter of minutes. A reading of 120/80 in a relaxed setting may rocket under pressure into the 145/95 above normal zone. This predisposition, known as "labile high blood pressure," affects a large number of adults. Only when your pressure is frequently and consistently elevated does it become true hypertension.

Hypertension and Heart Disease Causes

Anxiety and emotional stress elevate blood pressure in many individuals but not all. Tension is not always synonymous with hypertension, but studies do show that anxiety raises blood pressure. My entire wellness program contains various components that break anxiety.

The causes of so-called "essential hypertension" are an improper, poorly balanced diet, usually high in sodium and fat and low in the essential heart-protective nutrients: potassium, calcium, trace elements, and vitamins B, C and E. And the only "cure" is a total change in diet and habits.

Treating your condition with drugs creates a Catch-22 situation, often sending you into a downward spiral, making you vulnerable to other heart and vascular disturbances with other major organ disorders such as kidney and lung disease.

Psychological Factors in Hypertension

Anxiety levels are predictive of later incidents of high blood pressure and heart disease, according to the Framingham study. We believe that every individual with heart disease may have a hypertensive personality, and this we confirmed recently in an editorial by Thomas Pickering, "Tension and Hypertension," *JAMA* 370:20, p. 2494, 1993. See also, Markovitz, J., et al., "Psychological Predictors of Hypertension in the Framingham Study," *JAMA* 370:20, pp. 2439-42, 1993.

The *Journal of Hypertension,* July 1993, showed that individuals with undue stress also have high blood pressure. People who control their own schedule and own pace may seem to find less stress. It is not the work you do, but the amount of control that you feel over it, which makes the mercury move, according to the study. This is an unavoidable consequence. It is wise to be able to distinguish between the stresses that you can control and those that you cannot. It is the ones that you cannot control that seem to affect blood pressure. Again, this points to the same basic factor; namely, that we must understand our personalities and psychological stresses, and we must treat ourselves with CES, diet, nutrition, exercise, arrangement of our schedule, etc. Once we do this, our opportunities to reverse our high blood pressure and heart disease can improve greatly.

Chapter 9

Healthy Heart Quiz: Test Your Cardiovascular IQ

1. **Eggs contribute most to cholesterol elevations in the average person. True or false?**
   Answer. False. Saturated fat in the diet raises cholesterol more than cholesterol intake. Sugar and white flour also probably raise cholesterol as much as cholesterol intake. Eggs account for 35 percent of the cholesterol in the diet. Beef is next (16 percent). Up to seven eggs a week usually have little effect on blood cholesterol. Fish and poultry are preferable to beef, since too much beef can increase cholesterol. Eating cholesterol is not the problem; it is eating the wrong foods that cause the synthesis of cholesterol and deficiency of sex hormones, which results in the accumulation of cholesterol.

2. **The top ten sources of fat in the American diet are hamburgers, meat loaf (7.0 percent), hot dogs, ham, lunch meats (6.4 percent); whole milk (6.0 percent); doughnuts, cakes, cookies (6.0 percent); and fish (5.5 percent). True or false?**
   Answer. True for the first four, but beef, steak and roasts, not fish, are fifth.

3. **Meat alone accounts for 27 percent of the total fat and 33 percent of the saturated fat in the American diet. True or false?**
   Answer. True.

112

4. **Name two food oils that lower blood pressure.**
   Answer. Safflower oil and sunflower oil are great oils to lower pressure and cholesterol. In addition, they have a diuretic effect.

5. **If your blood pressure is normal, it should be checked every two years, then yearly after 50. True or false?**
   Answer. True.

6. **What four nutrients lower blood pressure best?**
   Answer. Linoleic acid (in polyunsaturated oils), fish oil, magnesium and garlic.

7. **Which of these vegetables is a source of unhealthy saturated fat?**
   a) avocado
   b) tomato
   c) eggplant

   Answer. a). The avocado is the *only* vegetable that's not so good for your heart. Eggplant helps *reduce* cholesterol; tomatoes do neither. If you love guacamole, use an avocado-free formula. If you make guacamole, substitute cooked puréed string beans.

8. **The three best sports for building cardiovascular fitness for life are swimming, bowling, and bicycling. True or false?**
   Answer. False, says the President's Council on Physical Fitness. Jogging or brisk walking are better than bowling.

9. **Which of the following foods does the American Heart Association suggest eating daily to keep your heart healthy?**
   a) eggs
   b) polyunsaturated oils
   c) bran

   Answer. b) and c). Safflower oil is preferable to other oils. If your blood pressure is over 140/80, use safflower oil.

10. **Which of the following foods and nutrients help prevent dangerous blood clots?**

a) capsicum hot peppers
b) spaghetti
c) potatoes
d) fish oil
e) garlic
f) vitamin E

Answer. a), d), e), f). According to the American Clinical Nutrition Society, hot peppers help activate anticlotting action in the blood. Regular pepper eaters in New Guinea, Bantu, Korea, East Africa, and Thailand have the lowest incidence of blood clots in all the world's people.

However, a small fraction of people may get arthritis-like symptoms from peppers. Fish oil, niacin, garlic, and vitamin E are the great heart vitamins.

11. **Sodium is an essential mineral you should reduce. Which essential mineral should you increase? And what is the best source?**

Answer. Calcium, says Dr. David A. McCarron, associate professor of medicine at the University of Portland.

Surveys of dietary habits in persons with high blood pressure indicate they consume significantly *less* calcium than those with normal blood pressure. Low-fat dairy foods, such as low-fat cottage cheese and yogurt, are a primary source of calcium, and both are available in low-sodium versions. Dark leafy green vegetables are a good source of calcium. Tofu is rich in calcium and can be used occasionally by people on a Plan A diet. Other studies suggest that magnesium is the key nutrient.

12. **Which blood pressure reading below indicates the highest risk of cardiovascular disease?**

a) above 140/90
b) below 140/90 but much lower on medication
c) between 110/70 and 120/80

Answer. b). Ironically if you lower your blood pressure too much you can be at increased risk.

13. **Visible light blue blood vessels on the back of your hand are soft and pulsating; what does this mean?**
    Answer. Your cardiovascular system is in good working order, says Dr. Edward Kowalewski, professor and chairman of family practice at the University of Maryland School of Medicine in Baltimore.
14. **What do red earlobes or a red nose sometimes indicate?**
    Answer. Circulatory problems, says Dr. Robert E. Mendelsohn, former associate professor of preventive medicine at the University of Illinois.
15. **Which supplies the most saturated fat?**
    a) imitation diet margarine
    b) liquid corn oil margarine (stick form)
    c) peanut oil
    Answer. b) and c) have 2 grams per tablespoon; a) has 1 gram.
16. **Which has more cholesterol?**
    a) coconut oil
    b) mayonnaise
    c) lard
    Answer. c). Lard has 13 mg per tablespoon; mayonnaise has 8; coconut has none (but it does supply saturated fat).
17. **Why do you use the index and middle fingers instead of the thumb to take your pulse?**
    Answer. Because the thumb has a pulse of its own. In some cases, pulse is a marker of heart health.
18. **If your pulse rate is over 120 when you stop exercising, what does this indicate?**
    Answer. That your routine was too intense or too long, unless you are young enough that your doctor says it's okay. Lighten up and always do cool-down exercises.
19. **Certain colors make you feel better and improve your blood pressure readings. True or false?**
    Answer. True, says Dr. Harry Wohlfarth, president of the Garan Academy of Color Science and a photobiologist at the University of Alberta in Canada. He explains, "It's

not the actual vision of the color that affects us, but the waves of electromagnetic energy that make up the colors." In one study, changing the colors in a classroom of handicapped children reduced blood pressure in several students. Healthiest colors are the low-key tones: black, blue and green. If color can do this, how much more can CES relax people? Read about CES in Chapter 12.

20. **The average heartbeat (at rest) for a man is 62, for a woman is 60. The best time to determine yours is to take your pulse for one full minute before you get up in the morning. True or false?**
    Answer. False. The average heart rate for a man is 72 and 80 for a woman. Many studies suggest that lower pulse rates, e.g., 50 for a male, may even be better.

SCORING

- Score 1 point for each correct answer.
- 20-15: Excellent
- 14 or less: Fair. Take a closer look at your diet and health habits.

Chapter 10

Heart and Vascular Testing

The Heart Charts:
The Basic Three Tests You
Need to Monitor Your
Cardiovascular Fitness

To keep track of your cardiovascular fitness, here are the basic three healthy heart charts you need to consult. It's simple—two out of the three you can *do yourself* if you have the right device.

ONE: Blood Pressure
Classification: 18 years and over.

DIASTOLIC: (the lower number)

- less than 89   *normal* blood pressure
- 90 to 104   *high normal* blood pressure (or borderline) *mild hypertension**
- 105 to 114   moderate hypertension
- 115 or more   severe hypertension (if symptoms are present, this is called "crisis hypertension")

SYSTOLIC: (the upper number and coupled with a diastolic reading of less than 90)

* Most hypertensives fall into this category.

■ less than 140   normal blood pressure
■ 140 to 159   borderline isolated systolic
                        hypertension
■ 160 or more   isolated systolic hypertension

What you need. Electronic and nonelectronic home blood pressure kits are available for $30 to $100 at medical pharmacies and from medical mail order suppliers.

TWO: Exercise Pulse Rates

Keep your heart rate in the low to middle area of the training range, when you exercise—this is about 70 to 75 percent of your aerobic capacity. To determine that rate, subtract your age from 220 and multiply the result by .60 and .75 for your target number of beats per minute.

Age	Target Zone
20	120–150
25	117–146
30	114–142
35	111–138
40	108–135
45	105–131
50	102–127
55	99–120
60	96–120
65	93–116
70	90–113

Exercise that sustains this target zone level for thirty minutes should be undertaken at least three times a week.

What you need. Electronic pulse meters are available for $40 to $120 at sporting goods shops.

THREE: Cholesterol
(milligrams per deciliter;
must include HDL, LDL and TG)

Age	Moderate Risk	High Risk
2–19	over 170	over 185
20–29	over 200	over 220
30–39	over 220	over 240
40 and up	over 240	over 260

Cholesterol levels are expressed in milligrams per deciliter of blood. Anything below 200 is good; 200 to 239 is considered "borderline" and may require treatment if you have other heart disease risk factors; 240 or above makes you a candidate for therapy right away.

Make sure you get an accurate reading of your number. The most accurate test is one in which a blood sample is drawn intravenously by a doctor or technician and processed in a hospital or commercial clinical laboratory.

What about the "instant" cholesterol tests where a drop of blood is obtained with a finger prick and analyzed in minutes by a machine that does essentially the same thing as a lab test? These widely available tests, even though they are not controlled and therefore may not provide a precise measurement, are useful. HDL takes cholesterol away from the heart and thereby protects against cancer and heart disease. HDL levels of 40 or greater are OK, but levels of 55-70 are better. Levels of 70-80 show extremely low heart disease risk. Levels between 15-30 indicate trouble perhaps a shortened life.

Some Tips

■ Fast for 12 hours. The longer you wait after eating, the better.

■ If your level is high, have another test a week or two

later, then base your treatment on the average of the two numbers. Also, test the ratio of the high-density lipoproteins to low-density lipoproteins.

■ Blood cholesterol blood readings over 260 quadruple your risk of developing heart disease (compared to levels of 190 or below).

What you need. If you have hypertension, your blood cholesterol levels should be measured twice a year or more by your doctor until they normalize.

Useful Supplementary Blood Tests

Apolipoproteins	A is like HDL
	B is like LDL (reveals genetic factors)
Serum fibrinogen	may reveal heart attack risk
Trace elements	especially RBC magnesium, zinc, chromium, selenium and copper levels
Amino acids	i.e., taurine
Essential fatty oils	evaluates saturated fat and fish oil polyunsaturates in the blood

Doppler Test

The Doppler test is a scientific way of determining how well your arteries and veins are circulating blood throughout your body. Arteriosclerosis is a disease in which plaques and clots build up in blood vessels and block blood flow to vital organs such as the heart and brain. This process can eventually result in heart attacks or strokes if it goes untreated for too long. *Fortunately, now with the Doppler test, blood supply to your brain, legs and arms can be accurately measured without side effects.* Segmental blood pressures can also assist identification of blood vessel blockages.

Procedure: There is no special preparation needed for this test. You may be asked to change into a loose-fitting gown in order to make it easier to perform the required measurements. First, blood pressures will be taken in your arms. Then you will lie down and four different pressures will be taken in each leg. An advanced computerized instrument will then accurately measure a tracing of your blood flow in your arteries and veins of the legs, arms and neck. The entire test may take about an hour since such extensive and thorough readings are needed. There are absolutely no needles used and the procedure is completely painless. In the best quality machines a color picture will be available for your review.

Purpose: Heart disease, strokes, kidney failure, high blood pressure, leg gangrene, venous phlebitis, varicose veins, leg edema (or swelling), cold hands or feet are just some of the conditions caused by circulation troubles. Hardening of the arteries, or atherosclerosis, is a gradual process of starving the body of oxygen since red blood cells carry cholesterol within the bloodstream. Sometimes symptoms such as chest pain or leg cramps (especially in the cold or after walking) can be symptoms of this process. Most of the time, however, there is no way to detect the process until it is so advanced that a serious medical problem results. The Doppler test is one of the few ways to detect any early signs of blood vessel disease even before it causes any damage. If discovered early, it is possible to reverse the process (with diet, nutrients, drugs and chelation) before it is too late.

Doppler Testing: Vascular Screening

New ultrasound machines are able to search virtually the entire arterial and vena system in the hands, feet, legs, arms, and neck for blockages. Individuals who are at risk for blockages are people with leg pains, cramps, nonhealing ulcers, leg swelling, varicosities, numbness, impotence, and change of skin color. Particularly at risk are hypertensive patients, diabetics, smokers, victims of stroke and TIAs (small strokes), geriatric patients, overweight patients, and pregnant women. The examination is very safe and painless. The procedure is done with photo cells, infrared light waves, and ultrasound (high frequency sound waves which record light reflections and sound waves in the arteries and veins). Sound waves and reflected light patterns are converted to signals which appear on a strip chart or television-like screen. From these wave forms it is possible to determine if blockages or clots are present.

During the exam, the patient should lie quietly and refrain from talking. Blood pressure cuffs can be placed and small probes can be taped to the fingers and toes during the exam. The blood pressure cuff will be inflated on a rotation basis and gives the physician information on the blood supply to the extremities.

Symptoms for arterial studies include absent or diminished pulses, claudication, wrist pain, vasospastic disease, ulcers, pre- and postoperative surgical evaluations. Venous studies can help give information on acute deep vein thrombosis, edema, pain, postphlebitic ulcers, high risk for pulmonary embolism, valvular incompetency, both deep and superficial systems, carotid cerebral studies, transient ischemic attacks (TIAs), asymptomatic carotid bruits, branchial blood pressure differences, diminished pulses, postendarterectomy follow-up.

Many diseases require this type of peripheral vascular study, including peripheral arteriolosclerosis and arteriosclerosis of any type, high cholesterol, Raynaud's syndrome, Buerger's disease, thoracic outlet syndrome, venous insufficiency, vasculogenic impotence, carotid artery stenosis, longstanding diabetes, claudication, ischemic ulcers, subclavian steal syndrome, phlebitis or thrombophlebitis, cerebral thrombosis, etc.

Tobacco, caffeine, and other vascular constrictors used shortly before testing may distort results. Cold hands or feet can produce falsely abnormal digit wave forms. The patient must lie quietly and not talk during the exam, and must try to reduce test tension for more accurate results.

Indications for Noninvasive Vascular Testing

ARTERIAL

Skin color changes or ulceration*
Preoperative and postoperative evaluation*
Diminishing/absent distal or pedal pulses*
Distal extremity hair loss (trophic changes)*
Intermittent claudication*
Leg pain, rest pain, night cramps*
Medical-legal documentation*
Gangrene*
Extremity weakness or fatigue*
Differentiation of various paresthesias
Diabetic neuropathy
Numbness
Positive Allen's Test
Coldness in an extremity
Raynaud's phenomenon
Thoracic outlet syndrome
Subclavian steal syndrome
Hypertension
Frostbite (cold injury)
Skin or nail infections
Lower extremity bone fractures
Cigarette smoking
Heart disease

* Most frequent indications

CEREBROVASCULAR-CAROTID

Cervical or carotid bruit*
Cluster-type headaches*
Lapse of memory
Loss of balance
Loss of vision
Visual disturbances
Transient ischemic attack (TIA—recovery within 24 hours)*
Vertigo*
Increased vessel wall rigidity found during palpation*
Unilateral paresthesias
Aphasia
Amaurosis fugax
Dizziness
Syncope
Dysarthria
Fluctuating confusion
Loss of memory
Motor deterioration
Bruit (murmur)
RIND (recovery > 24 hours)
Stroke
Ataxia
Drop attacks (sudden muscular weakness)

* Most frequent indications

VENOUS

Monitoring patients with high risk of venous
thrombosis*
Presence of pitting edema*
Varicose veins with symptoms*
Venous thrombosis and postphlebitic syndrome*
Skin color changes (Hemosiderin deposition)*
Extremity weakness or fatigue*
Pulmonary embolism
Oral contraceptive use
Ulcers
Cellulitis

---

* Most frequent indications

Vascular Patient History:
Risk Factors and Ideal Examination
for Peripheral Vascular Disease

Diagnosed conditions

Diabetes	_____ years
Hypertension	_____ years
Hyperlipidemia	_____ family history
Prev. vasc. surgery	Syncope
Stroke/TIA	Varicose veins
Heart disease	Impotence
Angina	Bruit (murmur)

Risk factors

Cigarette/tobacco use
   Years smoked: 0.0   PPD: 0.0
   Years quit: 0.0   pack years: 0
Sedentary
Oral contraceptives

Current symptoms

Gangrene	Edema
Leg hair loss	Paraaesthesia\weakness
Skin color changes	Burning sensation
Stasis dermatitis	Ulcerations
Trophic nails	Cyanosis
Cellulitis	Rubor
Absent PT pulse	Headaches
Absent DP pulse	Vertigo

Pulse Grade PT
Pulse Grade DP
Pulse Grade POP
Pulse Grade FEM
Rest Pain
Claudication

Pain at: thigh/buttock
       calf
       arch
       toe

Pain relief: rest
         exercise
         legs elevated
         legs down

Distance walked before pain (blocks)

EKG and Echocardiogram (Echo)

Every adult over the age of thirty should have an electrocardiogram (EKG) once a year and adults at high risk, twice a year. An electrocardiogram is an electrical tracing of your heart activity. It measures whether or not the pumping function of your heart is working efficiently, or if there is an electrical conduction delay resulting in uneven heart muscle contraction. It can tell if the different chambers of your heart are working in rhythm with each other or if they are "out of step." All sorts of irregular beats and their causes can be detected. In addition, the EKG can often detect whether you have had a "silent" heart attack in the past and can show if there are signs of an impending one. Finally, an enlarged or hypertrophied heart may show up as an abnormal tracing. A normal EKG can be a great reassurance that your heart is functioning well and working harmoniously with your body to contribute to your good health. This is especially true when the EKG has been analyzed by computer and/or accompanied by an echocardiogram. An echo is a safe ultrasound picture of the heart valves and functions and is a great predictor of heart size and pump efficiency. The echo, along with a PET (Positron Emission Tomography) test, is the only way to accurately assess subtle heart disease not seen or not understood by EKG.

High Triglycerides and High Cholesterol

Nutritional treatment of high triglycerides is very successful. Seven capsules daily of EPA can lower triglycerides from 800 to 150 (normal) in just six months. EPA (fish oil) lowers almost all forms of triglycerides. Niacin is also effective in lowering triglycerides (type 4) but the flushing may be uncomfortable (Willner, Bronson or other forms of timed release may eliminate this problem, but liver enzymes must be checked every 3 to 6 months). Diet is very important. Avoid sugar and alcohol, which frequently may do more to raise triglycerides than cholesterol levels. Saturated fat intake, e.g., cream, whole milk, frying or baking with oil, fatty meat and butter, should be reduced or eliminated. Fish daily and two tablespoons daily of safflower or sunflower oil (possibly olive oil if there is no hypertension) are very helpful. Supporting nutrients (selenium, chromium, magnesium, pantetheine, carnitine and evening primrose oil) are a helpful treatment of high triglycerides.

High cholesterol is more difficult to lower than high triglycerides. Most cholesterol levels go down with a reduction of refined carbohydrates. The same dietary approach as above is necessary. Sometimes red meat or even whole grains need to be reduced. Primrose oil or safflower oil (2 to 4 Tbsp. per day) is helpful. Lecithin may be helpful (2 to 10 Tbsp. per day). Olive oil may also be useful, especially in improving HDL ratios. Niacin and fish daily can also help. Arginine and methionine are amino acids that can lower cholesterol slightly. HDL—the good cholesterol—is raised by exercise, EPA (fish oil), garlic, carnitine, pantetheine, vitamin C, and niacin daily. One drink per day (not more) may also raise HDL, but the bad side effects of alcohol outweigh this one possible good effect. Other supporting nutrients are the same as for treating high triglycerides. Zinc and vitamin E in very large doses raise LDL levels (the bad form of cholesterol). Overall, antioxidants probably protect against the side effects of high cholesterol.

Causes of HighCholesterol Levels

1. Excess dietary sugar
2. Excess dietary starch
3. Excess hydrogenated or processed fats (lard, shortening, cottonseed oil, palm oil, margarine, etc.)
4. Liver dysfunction
5. Amino acid deficiency
6. Essential fatty acid deficiency
7. Deficiency of natural antioxidants such as vitamin E, selenium and beta-carotene

8. Increased tissue damage due to infection, radiation, or oxidative activity (free radicals, etc.)
9. Fiber deficiency
10. Vitamin C deficiency
11. Carnitine deficiency
12. Biotin deficiency
13. Food allergies
14. Alcoholism
15. Hormone deficiency (testosterone, DHEA, estrogen, etc.).

Causes of Low Cholesterol Levels

1. Immune decline
2. Chronic hepatitis
3. Cholesterol lowering drugs
4. Essential fatty acid deficiency
5. Liver infection or disease
6. Manganese deficiency
7. Adrenal stress
8. Street drugs (cocaine, marijuana, etc.)
9. Excessive exercise (especially in females)
10. Low fat diets
11. Psychological stress
12. Cancer

Positron Emission Tomography

Positron Emission Tomography, or PET scan, is an extremely useful technique using positive electrons that are attached to biochemical compounds which can be injected into the body and rapidly leave the body. In this short period of time, the body is exposed to a minimum level of radiation (2 hours). PET provides an ability to access the brain's chemistry and the body's circulation without a catheter or dye. We now

believe that PET scanning will completely replace cardiac an-
giography. This procedure is also more cost-effective in that
it costs $2000 rather than $5000, although insurance companies may be reluctant to pay for it. The PET scan may also
replace, to some degree, the stress test.

Low-level blockages in the blood vessels, i.e., only 50 percent, can now be detected by PET, rather than waiting for
blockages in the circulation to reach 75 to 90 percent, a level
detected by more conventional techniques such as stress testing and catheterization. Chelation, diet and nutrient therapy
may be techniques to reverse blockage.

Body Composition Analysis

Body composition analysis is an important way of evaluating
your muscle and body fitness. It will tell you the amount of
body fat that you have, suggest a goal weight, and help you
identify dietary ways in which you may improve your percentage of body muscle. It is also important for an individual to
follow body composition while dieting to make sure that he
does not lose muscle while dieting. Loss of muscle while dieting can be a very serious problem and affect your heart
muscle.

Body components change throughout our life. For example,
a fetus is 90 percent water, 0.6 percent fat, 6.3 percent protein,
while a premature child is typically anywhere between 82 to
86 percent water, 1 to 4 percent fat, 8 to 9 percent protein.
Yet a full-term child is 71 percent water, 13.5 percent body
fat and 12 percent protein. Most adult males tend to be 60
percent water, 17 percent body fat, and 18 percent protein,
with the remaining fractions being minerals. As we age we all
gain body fat. The ideal is probably 7 to 13 percent body fat.

If a person weighs 150 pounds and he has 20 percent body
fat, then he has 30 pounds of fat and 120 pounds of what is
referred to as lean mass. Muscle tissue increases or decreases

depending on a person's diet, activities, exercise and lifestyle. While the average American typically loses muscle and gains fat steadily from age 20, this does not have to be so, and weight training can actually benefit the body components as well as total volume with age, and it can benefit overall health. The average American male has the following proportions of body fat:

Age	Percentage of body fat
20	10.3%
25	13.4%
30	16.2%
35	18.6%
40	21.0%
45	22.0%
50	24.0%
55	25.0%

Though a person may weigh the same at age 65 as he did at age 30, his body may have deteriorated substantially in terms of muscle mass. This can be responded to so that dieting and exercise can lead to the rebuilding of this muscle tissue. The body muscle can be continually built up at any age if proper exercise and diet are followed. Composition measures show what the scales won't show, whether, when a person goes off his diet and gains the weight back, he is gaining more fat and less muscle than he had originally.

Measuring body fat regularly will determine the effectiveness of an exercise/diet program being used. It is probably harmful for a man's body to be any lower than 6 to 7 percent fat because then there would be no reserve.

Body fat measurements can help direct a person how to diet and exercise—how to recognize the need for better diet, calories and nutrition. Individuals who are correct height and weight may actually have too much fat. Many individuals who appear to still be overweight while dieting will actually have added muscle and lost fat. The scale cannot give this type of information. For individuals who may be redistributing, the body composition device can help tell whether or not a person actually is redistributing, that is, adding muscle and losing fat. For some people who diet, this may be beneficial. Measuring body fat with skin fold calipers is very accurate.

The ideal amount of body fat in men as they get older is probably about 12 percent, and for women, 15 to 18 percent.

Body Composition

Body Status	Percent Body Fat	Percent Lean Body Mass
Women Very low fat	9-17	91-83
Low fat	18-21	82-79
Average	22-25	78-75
Above average	26-29	74-71
High fat	30-35	70-65
Very high fat	35+	65-
Men Very low fat	6-10	94-90
Low fat	11-15	89-95
Average	16-18	84-82
Above average	19-20	81-80
High fat	21-25	79-75
Very high fat	25+	75-

Body fat is the reserve energy stored within body cells. This energy is measured in calories. For every 3500 calories consumed above the amount expended, the body creates one pound of fat. Serious health risks are associated with high body fat levels.

Lean body mass is fat-free weight composed of muscle, vital organs, body fluids, connective and other nonfat tissue. The greater the amount of muscle, the more efficiently the body metabolizes or "burns" fat. Dieting without exercise can result in the loss of 50 percent fat and 50 percent muscle, thus maintaining the same ratio of body fat to lean body mass.

Body fat is probably a good correlation to coronary artery blockages and overall health.

What Is Body Composition Analysis?

Body Composition Analysis (BCA) is an extremely sensitive and accurate way to determine the ratio between body fat and lean body mass. It does this with a new technology called impedance plethysmography. Because this procedure takes into account the actual makeup of the body, it is far more useful than simple weighing when on a weight-loss or improved fitness program. The BCA computer not only calculates the mass ratios, but also predicts the risk of cardiovascular disease and supplies specific suggestions for exercise and weight reduction. When this test is repeated monthly, you get a "moving picture" of your progress. This method is gaining wide acceptance by sports trainers, exercise physiologists and nutritionally oriented physicians.

To monitor your progress, you should schedule another BCA one month after your first. Tests should be repeated at monthly intervals until you reach your weight/exercise goal.

How to Prepare for the Test

Although it is exceedingly accurate, certain factors may affect your results. Therefore, it is important that you follow these directions in preparing for your BCA:

1. Minimize salt intake for at least 24 hours prior to the test.
2. Unless you regularly take diuretics (whether water pills or herbal preparations), do not take them.
3. No alcohol intake 24 hours prior to the test.
4. Women should not schedule their test during the week

before their periods. Follow-up tests should be scheduled at approximately the same time of the month as prior tests.
5. Do not eat for at least four hours prior to your test. You may, however, drink the normal amount of liquid customary for you.
6. Do not engage in strenuous aerobic exercise on the day of the test.

24-Hour Blood Pressure Monitor

The 24-hour blood pressure monitor is an exciting new breakthrough in the management of high blood pressure. We all know that blood pressure varies greatly at different times of the day and under different stress conditions. Many individuals (especially those with generalized anxiety who come to the doctor) have falsely elevated blood pressure ("white coat" hypertension). Although this elevation may be an indication of a predisposition for high blood pressure, it frequently does not need to be treated. A 24-hour blood pressure monitor is very helpful in measuring average blood pressure and elevated blood pressures. Elevated 24-hour blood pressures are very predictive of risk for left ventricular hypertrophy (LVH). This means that as blood pressure increases, the heart muscles have to work against more blood pressure, and the heart increases in size. An enlarged heart muscle is not good. For example, a person with big biceps is not able to pitch a baseball because he has an overly muscular arm. Therefore, you have to watch out for your heart becoming overly muscular as a result of high pressure. Fortunately, LVH is a reversible condition in many individuals.

The 24-hour blood pressure monitor is the ultimate in checking blood pressures; it measures a person's nighttime and daytime blood pressures and provides an average. In the future, the established 140/90 goal as a standard upper ceiling of normal blood pressure may need to be lowered. It seems prudent to say that the blood pressure that is best for a person is that blood pressure which will not result in increased cardiovascular disease, e.g., increase in heart size, heart attack or stroke. A lower blood pressure in age groups 40 to 70 (over 80 this may not be true), e.g., 120/80 or even 110/80, results in a reduction in total mortality. Yet when individuals with high blood pressure have their blood pressure lowered to these values by drugs, it certainly results in more deaths. Most drug treatments that lower pressure too much can be dangerous. If drugs are used, 140/90 is the goal pressure; without drugs, 120/80 or 110/70. The blood pressure monitor can also be used to help the doctor understand if blood pressure has been satisfactorily corrected through treatment. So there are basically five main uses:

1. Evaluate white coat hypertension.
2. General blood pressure evaluation.
3. Evaluation of the effect of drugs.
4. Evaluation of left ventricular hypertrophy. This condition may require an echocardiogram in addition to an EKG. It is also marked by strain of the heart and is one of the main problems associated with sudden death in heart disease.
5. Evaluation of the blood-pressure lowering effects of a nutritional diet and healthful lifestyle program.

Holter Monitors

Holter monitors are very useful for measuring heart rhythms over a 24-hour period. They can detect subtle arrhythmias and life-threatening arrhythmias, thus helping a physician decide which medication or even which nutritional approach might help. Holter monitors can also be utilized as event recorders. They frequently detect slow or sick sinus syndrome in adults who need pacemakers. Any patient with a potential cardiac arrhythmia history should utilize a Holter monitor.

Chapter 11

More Dietary Considerations for Hypertension and Heart Disease

Trimming the Fat

Substitute the following low-fat foods for high-fat ones.

High-Fat Food	Low-Fat Food
Whole or condensed milk	Skim milk, buttermilk, nonfat powdered milk
Bacon	Chicken (or Canadian bacon)
Bologna, frankfurter, sausage	Chicken or turkey, lean, thinly sliced
Avocado	Cucumber, zucchini, lettuce
Creamy or high-fat cheeses	Low-fat cheese, cottage cheese
Ice cream	Ice milk, frozen low-fat yogurt
Nuts	Fruits or vegetable snack

Hot fudge sundae	Frozen yogurt or ice milk with sliced or crushed fruit
Ground beef	Lean beef with all fat trimmed
Fatty pork (spare ribs, ground pork)	Well-trimmed lean pork (leg, ham, picnic)
Sour cream	Low-fat yogurt, imitation sour cream
Regular salad dressing	Reduced-calorie salad dressing, vinegar, lemon juice
Cream	Skim milk
Fried egg	Poached or baked eggs
Liver	Lean meat, chicken, fish

Defeating Sugar Cravings Is Essential to Heart Disease Prevention and Treatment

Sugar cravings in individuals suffering from hypoglycemia, diabetes and depressions have multiple origins. One biochemical study of sugar cravings suggests that decreases in the brain content of serotonin causes us to crave sugar. Serotonin is made from the amino acid tryptophan, and tryptophan supplementations frequently decrease sugar craving. High-protein diets with high tryptophan-to-carbohydrate ratio also reduce sugar cravings.

GTF (glucose tolerance factor) has been reported to regulate blood sugar. This vitamin is essential for both diabetics and hypoglycemics. GTF contains chromium, which is frequently reduced in the plasma of patients with sugar cravings as well as in patients with cardiovascular disease.

Glutamine has been suggested to be useful in treating sugar cravings because glutamine is converted into sugar rapidly. Glutamine reduces sugar cravings because it's like eating sugar.

In sum, sugar cravings (as well as depression) are treated with tryptophan and GTF. Supportive nutrients in carbohydrate cravings include B vitamins, zinc, inositol and even lithium therapy when this impulse disorder becomes unmanageable.

Oxy-Cholesterol in Food

Years ago the discussion around cholesterol in food began. Cholesterol was viewed as causing arteriosclerosis and being responsible for the formation of plaques. In the '60s and '70s, cardiologists recommended that their patients eat low-cholesterol foods and more polyunsaturated fatty acids. Linoleic acid became famous. The sales of products rich in this essential acid—especially diet margarines—were staggering.

However, research showed that cholesterol in itself is not necessarily the problem. Cholesterol that has combined with oxygen to form what is called oxy-cholesterol works like a saturated fat or a peroxide radical, causing damage to cells throughout the body.

Animal experiments were done with rabbits in which pure cholesterol as well as oxy-cholesterols were given. After 45 days, thickening of the intima of the aorta was observed in the oxy-cholesterol group. No thickening was observed in the rabbits that were given the pure cholesterol. The same experiment has been done with monkeys. Those results were the same. Radioactive labeled oxy-cholesterols showed that they were notably connected to the LDL's and VLDL's. There was practically no affinity toward the high-density lipoproteins.

Oxy-Cholesterol Foods

Bacon	Lard
Brains	Milk powder
Butter	Parmesan cheese
Cheese (grated)	Pork
Chips	Radiated food (gamma-radiation)
Egg products	Salami
Fast foods containing	
butter and eggs	

Eating-Out Tips

1. You will need to ask questions about how some of the food was prepared. What thickening and breading agent was used—corn starch or wheat? Are any spices, sugars or food additives added that you should avoid?
2. Choose a restaurant with a large variety of foods so you will have many choices. Call before going, and ask about the food and preparation methods.
3. You may need to bring your own salad dressing, crackers or bread.
4. Fast food restaurants need to be chosen carefully to avoid hidden additives and hidden sources of ingredients. It is difficult to get them to reveal a list of ingredients for the prepared dishes you choose.
5. Cafeterias may be a solution to eating out, but they may use sulfating agents, sugar and MSG on the foods to improve taste.
6. À la carte eating can give flexibility in choosing the items of food to eat.
7. Select meats, fish and poultry cooked simply, accompanied by steamed vegetables to be safe. A salad bar allows you to select the foods you can eat. Ask about sulfating agents first.

8. When going out to a cocktail or a dinner party, contact your host and ask what's being served. You may need to being some munchies of your own. This is especially important for children's birthday parties. Make a small cake or suitable treat with a candle in it for your child to bring along.

The Problem of Vegetarianism

Many people throughout the world adopt a vegetarian diet for a variety of reasons, avoiding meat and, in some cases, all animal products such as eggs and milk. It is beyond the compass of this book to address the religious and ethical considerations involved in vegetarianism, but we feel that some comment on its adoption for reasons of health is relevant here, as it presents problems with respect to an adequately balanced intake of amino acids.

Epidemiologists have suggested that true vegetarian societies cannot adapt to stress adequately. Most vegetable proteins have amino acid deficiencies and are thus unsatisfactory as a sole source of protein; usually, lysine, methionine, tryptophan and threonine are deficient. These deficiencies can be overcome in part by the addition to the diet of other proteins rich in these amino acids. Although the essential amino acids may be adequate in a vegetarian diet, many other protien products may be deficient, e.g., peptides.

Many vegetables are toxic, such as cabbage and beans, which have an antithyroid effect. Part of the problem in a vegetarian diet is not in the toxins in the vegetables, but in the deficiencies they induce. If inadequately cooked, many legumes, including soybeans, lima beans, navy beans and peanuts, contain trypsin inhibitors. These interfere with the digestion of the protein and availability of the limiting amino acid, methionine. A 1979 article in *Nutrition Reviews* suggests that children less than two years old, on a vegetarian diet, are shorter and lighter than other children. Several studies suggest that reduced growth is due to zinc and calcium deficiencies. Vegan (pure vegetarian) diets are well below recommended calcium requirements for females. Lacto-ovo-vegetarians, who eat eggs and milk, seem to have less deficiency in zinc, calcium and vitamin D.

Meat, fish, fowl and liver are concentrated sources of vitamins E, A and B complex. Furthermore, animal foods are loaded with iron, zinc and other nutrients. It has been suggested that for lack of these nutritional advantages, vegetarians throughout history have not coped with stress as well as meat eaters.

The advantages of a high-vegetable diet are due to increased fiber and beta-carotene, which protect against cancer, particularly colon cancer. A high-vegetable diet is undoubtedly healthful, but probably should not exclude meat and other proteins. The ability to degrade fiber increases in high-meat diets. It has been shown that beef protein, even when present in up to 55 percent of the diet, will not raise cholesterol levels in normal men. It has been suggested that the real danger of high-protein, high-meat diets is that they are frequently accompanied by high consumption of refined carbohydrates. A diet high in vegetables, whole grains and lean meat may be the best.

The great contribution of vegetarianism is that it has made us aware of the need to eat more vegetables and fruit and less refined carbohydrates and junk foods.

B6 AND ZINC DEFICIENCY AND VEGETARIANISM

Zinc is an important nutrient that may be lacking in a vegetarian diet. Most vegetarians not only avoid meat, a good source of zinc, but increase their consumption of foods rich in phytates (beans, legumes and grains) which cause the elimination of zinc, calcium and other minerals in the digestive system; this can become a major problem. However, the addition of leaven or yeast to grains, as in leavened bread, destroys the phytates by fermentation; sprouting also destroys phytates. Sprouted grains, beans and seeds are most nutritious and should be a part of everyone's diet.

One patient from a southern city found that she could not eat any protein food such as fish, chicken or red meat without developing a feeling of unreality, dizziness and even hallucinations. Without fail she was unduly suspicious of her companions whenever she ate meat—she had paranoia.

She thought she had an allergy to all proteins. She came to the Brain Bio Center for food allergy testing, but on the initial tests we found her to be pyroluric, with a high kryptopyrrole level in her urine. We next found her to be deficient in zinc, manganese and vitamin B6, as are most pyroluric patients. Manganese, zinc and B6 are needed by the body to handle protein foods. With administration of these nutrients, she found that she could tolerate proteins for the first time in many years. She also started losing her excess body fluids and fat, dropping fifteen pounds in two months; her old dresses began to fit again.

I bring up this case because it is similar to those of many disperceptive teenagers, who when stressed find that paranoid symptoms increase after a protein meal. They feel better on an all-vegetable diet and so may not only eat as vegetarians but also join one of the many cults which espouse vegetarianism. A less drastic answer to their protein intolerance is typically zinc, 15 to 30 mg per day; vitamin B6 to the point of dream recall (often 1 g); and manganese, 50 mg each morning (of course, after consulting a physician). With these supplements they can again tolerate and enjoy protein foods.

REDUCING ALLERGY TO PROTEIN

We have become extremely limited in the kinds of meat we eat. Most eat beef, lamb, pork, chicken and turkey. Overuse of one protein can produce allergies to that protein.

When we eat different kinds of fish as a main source of protein, knowing that each fish protein is antigenically unique, we have an unlimited source of varied proteins if we are allergic to animal protein. Occasionally, kosher meat helps the meat-allergic individual. The koshering process removes blood in which the hemoglobin is antigenic and may cause immune complexes to form after absorption by the body.

THE HEALTHIEST CHOICE

If sufficient vegetables, whole grains and fish are eaten, the hazards of meat (produced organically) are probably canceled out. Some meat is necessary for resistance to stress. But excess meat and fat are to be avoided since they are implicated in cancer and heart disease. The threats to our meat and fish supply such as steroids, PCBs, antibiotics or hormones should be reduced or eliminated. But until that goal is reached, the nutrients such as cysteine that protect us against those hazards should be increased in our diets. In sum, meat diets should be high in vegetables, whole grains, fish and supplemental nutrients. We think that this combination is the one that leads to optimum health for most people.

PROBLEMS WITH VEGETARIANISM

Problems with vegetarianism are:
1. Inadequate warming of the body in some cases.
2. Inadequate in essential amino acids for the brain.
3. Second and third generations of vegetarians may have lower intellectual functioning and possibly impaired immune system functioning.

CARDIAC PATIENTS AND A VEGETARIAN DIET

Some cardiac patients, however, probably would do well on a strict vegetarian diet. By following such an eating regimen they would not have to make determinations about cholesterol intake or saturated fats—no gram counting, no choices, no opportunity to cheat.

Dr. Joel Fuhrman, our consultant in therapeutic fasting, has designed just such a vegetarian diet which could meet the needs of cardiac patients:

DR. FUHRMAN'S STRICT VEGETARIAN DIET

Breakfast: 2 grapefruit or melons

Lunch: Whole grapefruit, orange or melon

Large green salad — lettuce, snow peas, tomato, cucumber, stringbeans, shredded carrot, red pepper

Vegetable soup — all vegetables

More fruit — apple, kiwi, pears, banana, strawberries

Dinner: Steamed vegetables — green stringbeans, broccoli, zucchini, asparagus, artichoke

Starchy vegetables — potato, sweet potato, butternut, acorn squash

Brown rice

Carrots and peas

Whole-grain cereal/ lentils

NO dairy, milk, chicken, turkey, meat, oils or fats of any kind, nuts or seeds or sweets except for fresh fruit and fruit juices.

I would prescribe a regimen of nutritive supplements for any patient following this diet.

The Much-Maligned Egg: The Best Amino Acid Food

Heart disease often involves obstruction of the coronary arteries by fatty plaques which consist mainly of cholesterol. Cholesterol combines with calcium to become hard, hence the term "hardening of the arteries." The plaque which accumulates on the walls reduces arterial volume and results in higher blood pressure and harder work for the heart.

A well-proven strategy to prevent heart disease is to reduce dietary cholesterol intake. The overall rate of cholesterol intake in this country has dropped from 800 mg/day to less than 500 mg/day in the last ten years. At the same time, consumption of the "good" unsaturated fats and olive oil has increased by 60 percent. These changes in diet have done more to reduce heart disease than all medical procedures combined, according to Robert Levy of Columbia University.

Changes in cholesterol consumption have come mainly from reduction in meat intake, which is 40 percent less than ten years ago. Egg consumption has dropped only 12 percent, so it is apparent that the reduction in eggs has made little contribution to the decrease in heart attacks. In spite of the almost universal advice to limit their consumption because of their high cholesterol content, we think it is good to eat eggs because the egg is a nearly perfect amino acid food. Furthermore, the egg, because of its high lecithin content and other nutrients, does not raise blood cholesterol levels by more than 2 percent. To consider cholesterol content only is misleading because the ratio of cholesterol to other nutrients is what is important. This is the reason why Dr. John Yudkin was able to show that sugar and junk foods raised blood cholesterol levels, despite their low cholesterol content.

Most foods are of lower quality as protein sources than the

egg, which is proportionally the most balanced and best source of the essential amino acids. In each food, only one or two essential amino acids are deficient or totally lacking, and these are called the "limiting amino acids" for that food. The protein in that particular food will be usable by the body only to the extent that the limiting amino acid is present in another food being ingested at the same time. The egg's superior balance makes its protein more usable than those of most other foods.

Careful study of the effect of egg proteins on plasma amino acids shows that egg, like steak, raises lysine, valine, threonine and leucine to extremely high levels. Yet, the ratio to other amino acids is slightly better balanced with the egg than with steak. For example, steak increases the plasma valine-to-plasma methionine ratio to more than five to one, while for egg it is only four to one. The egg is slightly better balanced, but not perfectly balanced. Amino acid formulas are now being studied, which may suggest ways to achieve a more balanced rise in plasma amino acids than food itself can provide. At present, the egg is probably the best amino acid food source.

Potential Cancer Fighters in Foods Are Also Heart Disease Fighters

Although no food or food combination has yet been clinically proven to prevent or retard cancer in people, animal and test-tube research strongly suggests that many components have specific biological actions that may prove helpful. Scientists suspect that to treat tumors, compounds would have to be extracted or synthesized and given in larger doses than those found naturally; on the other hand, extracts or synthesis might overlook protective compounds in a healthy, varied diet. *Plaque growth is in some sense benign tumor growth.*

COMPONENT	POSSIBLE DISEASE-FIGHTING PROPERTIES	FOOD SOURCES
Allelic sulfides	May protect against carcinogens by stimulating production of a detoxification enzyme, glutathione S-transferase.	Garlic and onions
Carotenoids (Vitamin A precursors)	Antioxidants and cell differentiation agents (cancer cells are nondifferentiated)	Parsley, carrots, winter squash, sweet potatoes, yams, cantaloupe, apricots, spinach, kale, turnip greens, citrus fruits
Catechins	Antioxidants, linked to lower rates of gastro-intestinal cancer, mechanisms not understood.	Green tea berries
Flavonoids	Block receptor sites for certain hormones that promote cancers.	Most fruits and vegetables, including parsley, carrots, citrus fruits, broccoli, cabbage, cucumbers, squash, yams, tomatoes, eggplants, peppers, soy products, berries

COMPONENT	POSSIBLE DISEASE-FIGHTING PROPERTIES	FOOD SOURCES
Genistein	In test tubes, blocks angiogenesis, growth of new blood vessels essential for some tumors to grow and spread, and deters proliferation of cancer cells.	Found in urine of people with diets rich in soybeans and to a lesser extent in cabbage family vegetables
Fiber	Dilutes carcinogenic compounds in colon and speeds them through digestive system, thus discourages growth of harmful bacteria while bolstering healthful ones; may encourage production of healthier form of estrogen.	Whole grains and many vegetables
Indoles	Induce protective enzymes.	Cabbage, Brussels sprouts, kale
Isothiocyanates	Induce protective enzymes.	Mustard, horseradish, radishes

COMPONENT	POSSIBLE DISEASE-FIGHTING PROPERTIES	FOOD SOURCES
Limonoids	Induce protective enzymes.	Citrus fruits
Linolenic acid	Regulates prostaglandin production.	Many leafy vegetables and seeds, especially flaxseed
Lycopene	Antioxidants.	Tomatoes, red grapefruit
Monoterpenes	Some antioxidant properties; inhibits cholesterol production in tumors; aid protective enzyme activity.	Parsley, carrots, broccoli, cabbage, cucumbers, squash, yams, tomatoes, eggplant, peppers, mint, basil, citrus
Phenolic acids (tannins)	Some antioxidant properties; inhibit formation of nitrosamine, a carcinogen, and effect enzyme activity.	Parsley, carrots, broccoli, cabbage, tomatoes, eggplant, peppers, citrus fruits, whole grains, berries
Plant sterols (Vitamin D precursors)	Differentiation agents.	Broccoli, cabbage, cucumbers, squash, yams, tomatoes, eggplant, peppers, soy products, whole grains

COMPONENT	POSSIBLE DISEASE-FIGHTING PROPERTIES	FOOD SOURCES
Vitamin C	Antioxidant, inhibits creation of nitrosamine, a potentially dangerous carcinogen in the stomach.	Citrus fruits, tomatoes, green leafy vegetables, potatoes
Vitamin E	Antioxidant.	Wheat germ, oatmeal, peanuts, nuts, brown rice

Source: Dr. Christopher W. W. Beedner, *Eating Well Magazine.*

Diet and Anticoagulants

While you are on anticoagulant therapy you should eat less of the following foods that contain vitamin K:

Broccoli	Cabbage	Cauliflower	Kale
Kiwi fruit	Liver	Onions (fried	Papaya (raw)
Pineapples	Salad greens	or boiled)	Spinach
(raw)	Green tea	Soy meal,	
Turnips		soybean oil	

You should not drink any of the following:

Caffeine (coffee, tea, cola, etc.) Alcohol

Caution: Cooking oils that contain silicone additive will decrease absorption of your anticoagulant medication.

Magnesium

Magnesium is one of the most critical elements and is involved in over 300 enzymes in the body. Magnesium is needed for growth, pregnancy, sleep, wound healing, cardiac function, muscle function. Magnesium deficiency has been associated with seizures, psychosis, delirium, tremors, heart attacks, heart arrhythmia, premenstrual tension, osteoporosis, abnormal calcium deposits, poor wound healing, hypertension of pregnancy, difficult pregnancy, difficulty swallowing, etc. Magnesium has some natural tranquilizing abilities and has been used as a natural anticonvulsant and a natural antiarrhythmic. Its deficiency is associated with brittleness of bones and teeth because it is so important for calcium absorption. Magnesium deficiency can be associated with hypoglycemia. Loss of magnesium occurs with trauma, surgery, and extreme athletic competition. Alcoholics frequently are deficient in magnesium. The best way to measure magnesium is probably red blood cell and white blood cell magnesium levels. Even when these are normal, magnesium as a supplement or therapeutic agent above and beyond normal levels can be useful, particularly in hypertension, PMS, seizure disorders, depression, constipation, chronic fatigue and cardiac arrhythmia.

Many forms of magnesium, such as magnesium citrate, are used to clean out the bowels before sigmoidoscopy or barium enema. Magnesium oxide is a good supplement while milk of magnesia or magnesium hydroxide is a good antacid as well as laxative but not the best as a nutritional supplement. Chelated magnesium is expensive and probably no better than other forms of magnesium for absorption. Dolomite, which includes magnesium carbonate and calcium carbonate, may have toxins and does not have vitamin D, B6, or other nutrients which help in absorption. Magnesium silicate may result in silicate kidney stones. Magnesium orotate and gluconate have hardly any magnesium, and the former is not valuable except for its orotate content.

The best forms of magnesium are probably oxide from the hydroxide or chelated magnesium. Magnesium's uses have become so critical and better understood that it is now frequently used in emergency rooms around the country and in the intensive care and coronary care units because it is recognized that magnesium deficiency occurs commonly in patients on Digoxin, with heart attacks, and with rare arrhythmia such as torsades de points. Magnesium is a therapeutic agent that is becoming more and more widespread in medicine. Eventually, a new table salt using magnesium and other trace elements will probably be developed so that we get adequate magnesium from our environment, rather than too much sodium. Magnesium supplements help maintain adequate potassium supplementation in diuretic therapy and Bartter's syndrome. The diuretic Lozol may be somewhat magnesium sparing, although most diuretics result in increased magnesium loss.

MAGNESIUM AND BYPASS

Magnesium has been used to aid recovery after coronary bypass operations. A Boston study in 1992 tracked 100 bypass patients, half of whom were given an injection of magnesium chloride after surgery, with the other half being injected with a placebo. Sixteen percent of the magnesium group suffered heart-rhythm problems, while more than twice as many—34 percent—of the placebo group experienced such problems.

Chapter 12

Other Significant Topics: Stress, Relaxation, Sex, Hormonal Factors, etc.

Psychological Factors in Hypertension

It is well established that anxiety is the big predictor of hypertension. Personalities, of course, relate to heart disease in general. It is no surprise that Xanax and antianxiety drugs have been shown to help patients with heart disease. It's almost better to become addicted to things like Xanax and alcohol to relieve anxiety than eat yourself alive with anxiety.

Nervousness and elevation of sympathetic nervous system tone are indications of high risk for heart disease. This is why it is so critical to include biofeedback and CES on a regular basis, which can relieve anxiety and has FDA approval. Xanax, of course, in the long run is not the best way to relieve anxiety, neither is Dilantin or other drug techniques although Dilantin may be one of the better techniques in the long run. Biofeedback is one of the great ways to do it. Being quiet, being still, learning basic prayer and meditative techniques is another critical, long-term approach to hypertension. Anything that relieves anxiety on a daily basis is going to add up over time and transform the health-protecting immune system.

CES is probably the best of these things since it also antidotes the anxiety-causing side effects of the electromagnetic fields that we're all being exposed to. Electromagnetic fields cause brain waves to go from alpha to theta and lose their basic relaxing state.

Reversing Heart Disease and Hypertension

Recently homocysteine has received a lot of attention. Homocystine is an amino acid that as a sulphur amino acid is somewhat toxic. B6 is the way to antidote the occurrence of this toxic amino acid, which is a breakdown product of methionine. If you are taking methionine and not enough B6, you might contribute to your heart disease. As long as you take your B6 you should be in good shape. In terms of its measurability it is not so easy to measure and some of the routine amino acid profiles are not accurate. We are looking at the other profiles which should be accurate, and it is a good predictor of heart disease risk, yet if you are taking adequate B6, you shouldn't have any homocysteine.

Vitamin C might be important, as well as folic acid and B complex, to lowering homocysteine. In some cases, folic acid and B12 deficiency have been associated with homocysteine appearance. It is a good marker, maybe even a more accurate marker than cholesterol, for heart disease.

After all this hype over the years about cholesterol and homocysteine, studies still seem to suggest that your blood level of vitamin E may be your single, best predictor of heart disease risk, and it is very, very important that we all take advantage of vitamin E and fish oil, which help preserve the high levels of vitamin E, as well as vitamin C. Maybe we all should be taking 400 to 800 units of vitamin E.

Cardiac Reversal

The PATH chelation program for individuals with circulatory blockages has been very successful. We chose chelation after careful consideration of alternative methods. Carotid endarterectomy, a surgical technique, was once heralded as an advance in the treatment of cardial perfusion deficiencies. It is now reviewed as both dangerous and ineffective as a long term treatment. Mevacor and vitamin therapy all have potential. We will keep abreast of developments in these, as yet unproven, therapies. Chelation remains the best process for reversing vascular blockages, and we have been very successful in its use.

As a diagnostic tool, our investment in new Doppler equipment has been a great aid in assisting the identification of extremity vascular blockages.

INSURANCE COMPANY PUSHES CARDIAC REVERSAL AS TREATMENT OF CHOICE

While the concepts of new ideas, miracles and insurance companies are typically not found in the same story, we are very pleased to report that Mutual of Omaha, the largest medical insurance company in the United States, recently announced that cardiac bypass surgery would no longer be routinely approved until their insured patients had been evaluated for the suitability of entry into a program of noninvasive cardiac reversal. Although the initial focus will rely heavily on dietary changes, we believe that the use of nutrition, medication and chelation will become increasingly important and will gain wider public recognition from other insurers as well. As growing numbers of patients demand these noninvasive services, can the field of medicine be far behind?

The PATH program for cardiac reversal has been very successful. Numerous patients have documented through PET scanning and/or cardiac catheterization the reversal of previously blocked coronary arteries on the PATH reversal program. Other PATH patients have had increases in their collateral circulation.

PATH physicians are working in concert with the new insurance movement to educate consumers to alternatives to invasive procedures. We stand ready to help your friends, relatives and colleagues who may have cardiac or circulatory blockages to reverse them now to reduce their suffering and to avoid future problems.

Cholesterol Update

A new research study in the *Postgraduate Journal* reports that a cholesterol-lowering drug, when combined with nicotinic acid, had more benefit than when the two were used separately. Significant changes were observed in the cholesterol and the HDL ratio. It is thought that when the HDL/cholesterol ratio is 2.5 or less, cardiac reversal occurs. The report that a drug when combined with a vitamin had more significant effects than either alone is very significant and further supports the PATH medical approach that combines wellness, lifestyle changes and nutrition along with the best of modern conventional medicine. This combinational benefit has also been demonstrated in the use of antidepressants or psychiatric medication in combination with vitamin therapy.

Anger and Physical Health

An important concept for people on the path to wellness was recently advanced: Both anger and aggression contribute to the development of blockages in the large vessels supplying blood to the brain, the carotids, and likely impact other blood vessels throughout the body. Clearly, mental health and cardiovascular health are closely linked. The most effective way to deliver medicine today is to focus on both mental and physical health together. This is the PATH to Wellness concept, the new PATH in medicine. PATH is very committed to this concept, and that is why chelation, in conjunction with psychotherapy and biofeedback techniques that assist in reducing anger and aggression, is often recommended.

Recent studies reported in the *Journal of the American Medical Association* show that anxiety levels alone are predictive of high blood pressure. This is extremely important because it means that heightened anger intensities,. suppression of anger and anxiety in general, all contribute to high blood pressure. Modern medicine has directed its treatment efforts towards the use of drugs to treat the symptoms of high blood pressure. Sadly, physicians have generally missed the opportunity to transform patients' cardiovascular risks by treating high blood pressure at its origin, the central nervous system. Adjustment of the neurotransmitters in patients with hypertension and heart disease is critical to long-term cardiovascular reversal and the patient's ability to remain in an effective treatment program. The PATH staff understands the role that anxiety and psychological stress has in high blood pressure. That's why all of our patients now undergo Millon screening to allow us to identify the stress factors in their disease state. We will never again allow ourselves to miss the opportunity to heal the total person, both psychologically and physically at the same time.

Cranial Electrical Stimulation (CES)

Cranial electrical stimulation (CES) is a therapeutic procedure using minute battery-powered electronic stimulation for the purpose of inducing a relaxed state for the treatment of stress-related disorders: anxiety, depression and insomnia.

Cranial Electrotherapy Stimulation is done with a Transcutaneous Electric Nerve Stimulator (TENS) used on the head. It has been used for healing muscles, and, as an FES, or fine electrical stimulator, it enables stroke patients to open their hands. Electricity can be used for healing heart rhythms and healing bones. A technique developed by Dr. Braverman will change brain rhythms back to normal without the use of drugs. CES is FDA permitted and can be used as a primary treatment in anxiety, depression, and insomnia. Many publications show its benefit in anxiety, depression, insomnia, and even drug abuse in which anxiety and depression are frequently a part. CES is a safe, tested and proven therapy for:

Anxiety: an average improvement of over 50 percent in test scoring of hospitalized psychiatric patients and inpatient alcoholics with measured anxiety.

Stress-Related Withdrawal Syndrome: reduced stress measure, in every instance, by at least 40 percent for inpatient substance abusers related to withdrawal syndrome.

Depression: an average reduction of 50 percent in the depression score of long-term psychiatric patients, university counseling center clients, post-withdrawal alcoholic patients and hospitalized para- and quadriplegics.

Insomnia: significant improvement in sleep onset time, sleep efficiency, percentage of bedtime sleep, percentage of sleep time in stages one and four and percentage of delta sleep.

Additional research by Dr. Braverman with the BEAM machine suggests that CES, when worn on the forehead and left wrist over the radial pulse, is effective for daily use and will change brain rhythm without injuring the brain, like ECT (electroconvulsive therapy), because it is gentle electrical stimulation.

Why the left wrist? Possibly because of the transportation of electricity through the bloodstream to the left vagus nerve where studies suggest implanted CES devices can control brain rhythm.

Why the forehead? Possibly because the right brain is important to brain rhythm. CES is not a replacement for all drugs, but it is another useful medical technique for reducing anxiety when used frequently.

CES is safe and noninvasive. It is nonaddictive and has no pharmaceutical side effects. It is easy to use, and involves the simple nonirritating placement of electrodes. CES is efficient, comfortable, convenient, compact and portable for easy transport.

RECOMMENDED TREATMENT REGIMEN

As prescribed and monitored by the health professional: once a day for 30 to 60 minutes or more depending on physician and treatment goals. Some patients with severe addictions and depression may require 4 to 8 hours daily.

Although CES treatment is not known to be harmful to patients with any present disorder, it may be contraindicated in those patients known to be epileptic or pregnant. It should not be used on patients suffering from brain tumor and stroke.

HISTORY AND USAGE

Cranial electrical stimulation has a long history. The use of electricity in therapeutic disorders dates back in scientific history to Anton Mesmer, who tried to use magnetism for a variety of medical problems. Allen Childs, M.D., Assistant Professor of Pharmacy at the University of Texas at Austin, suggests that electrical therapies actually date back to ancient Egypt. Currently acceptable electrical uses include the TENS or Transcutaneous Electrical Nerve Stimulation device for pain, and variations on the TENS (FES or fine electrical stimulators) are used for some stroke patients.

Electrical currents have been experimented with for hard-to-heal bone fractures. There are also now brain or cranial TENS devices (CES) which seem to impact brain chemistry in many significant ways. Cranial electrical stimulation (CES) devices are thought to raise alpha waves, raise blood levels of endorphins and increase conversion of amino acids into the brain's neurotransmitters. The FDA has approved CES devices for anxiety, depression, insomnia and stress. The usual treatment can be 15, 30, or 60 minutes twice daily for stress; often individuals wear it overnight with a timer. At first comfort level may be exceeded after the first ten minutes. A poor connection or too high a dose can be discomforting and should be avoided. Poor electrode placement with reapplication can suddenly give a slight but uncomfortable shock. The device does possess an automatic shut-off valve. The intensity of current should be set at a comfortable level and the electrodes can be placed firmly on the mastoid process, forehead or arm. New studies suggest the best placement of electrodes will be near the left hand over the wrist or the forehead and above the nose. We are collecting data to evaluate precise location. If headache or any side effect occurs, the CES is discontinued. Pacemakers are contraindicators for use of the device.

Other possible applications of the CES are menstrual cramping, stiff neck, allergic reactions, headache, temporal lobe disorders, etc. The bioelectrical approach may be useful to modulate neurotransmitters in the brain so that they may rebalance the immune system and help with aspects of all depression and anxiety type symptoms. Patients who first use the cranial electrical stimulation device can often experience benefit in the first 30-minute session. Often a good marker of its benefits is that it will produce good relaxation and even improve sleep. For other individuals, an appropriate trial may be concurrent use with amino acids or antidepressants, which require at least three weeks to reach their full effect, and sometimes as much as two months to reach the full benefit.

The current of the CES device is one milliamp at 100 hertz (cycles/second) and 20 percent duty cycle. TENS units are 2 to 50 milliamps. To put this in perspective, wall sockets have 10 amps, or ten times the voltage, 60 hertz 110 volts.

Cranial electrical stimulation may be a very useful alternative to drug treatments in individuals who have treatment-resistant anxiety and/or depression. Furthermore, CES used in combination with the natural amino acids may convert the amino acids more rapidly to neurotransmitters resulting in greater effectiveness. The TENS device in combination with amino acids is also more effective than amino acid augmentation alone. Therefore, there is hope that this new approach, or brain bioelectrical approach, can be extremely successful and may actually become a first line therapy for psychiatric disorders because of its noninvasiveness and low level of side effects. It should be noted that individuals using this device may initially feel a tingling sensation. This is a good and normal reaction. It has been noted that the device has been experimented with by many other individuals and it has been called by some cerebral electrical therapy or CET, which started in the USSR in 1947. Treatment was done for 30 minutes, and double-blind studies were done. Again, frequency was at 100 cycles per second and pulse duration of 1 millisecond. There were changes in 24-hour urinary free catecholamines and 17 ketosteroid levels. Researchers have experimented with other cranial electrical devices and called them neurotonic therapy or neuroelectrical therapy (NET). Many researchers all around the country are actively studying the device, and I am sure our ability to use it effectively will continue to grow.

In summary, Cranial electrical stimulation (CES) is the FDA's term for any application of 1.5 ma or less of electricity across the head for medical purposes. Its use requires a prescription. Currently, all approved devices give 100 hertz, 0.5-1 milliamp, on a 20 percent cycle. Having followed recommendations of the National Research Council and after over

20 years of medical experience with CES in America, the FDA now considers the side effects of CES to be nonsignificant. For that reason their policy is not to require an Investigational Device Exemption prior to experimental studies of CES.

CES began in Europe in the 1950s under the rubric "Electrosleep." Eastern nations soon picked it up as a treatment modality, and its use had spread worldwide by the late 1960s when animal studies of CES began in the U.S. at the University of Tennessee and at what is now the University of Wisconsin Medical School. These were soon followed by human clinical trials at the University of Texas Medical School in San Antonio, the University of Mississippi Student Counseling Center, and the University of Wisconsin Medical School. As of April 1990, there were over 100 published CES studies appearing in the American literature.

Open marketing of the CES device began in the early 1970s in the U.S. for the clinical conditions of anxiety, depression and insomnia. Under the 1976 Medical Devices Amendment, the FDA grandfathered CES devices, which are currently marketed as previously, but limited to the earlier treatment claims until such time as a Premarket Approval Application is submitted to FDA for these and/or any additional treatment claims.

To date, several thousand Americans are treated with CES annually and more than 11,000 persons own CES devices, which have been prescribed for their home use. Possibly the most exciting application of the CES is for drug addiction. Further studies are needed to fully document use of the device for this purpose. In this technological age when we are surrounded by electromagnetic fields and currents, CES treatment may be necessary as an antidote and for maintenance of fully optimum health. Electromagnetic "pollution" from video screens, televisions, stereophonic equipment, microwaves and phone lines may be destroying our health and may require a device of this type. In addition, CES also probably incorporates some of the benefits of electroconvulsive or shock therapy (ECT) without the damaging effects of high amounts of current. CES probably provides natural levels of supplementary current to keep the brain healthy in the electrical age.

Biofeedback: Reducing the Stress of Heart Disease

Many states of illness tend to occur following major stressful events in our lives. Some examples include loss of a job or death of a loved one. In addition, preexisting diseases may worsen, such as an increase in high blood pressure or more frequent attacks of colitis or irritable bowel. This is because the state of our mind contributes to the state of our physical health. Modern medicine is beginning to recognize that all disease is partly psychosomatic—that is, our outlook and anticipation of the future strongly influence the course of our wellness or sickness.

The ability to deal with stress is an important tool in maintaining our sense of mental proportion. If we "fall apart" under pressure, we may be subject to frequent anxiety attacks, hyperventilation, painful muscle spasms, heart palpitations, or even the more long-term side effects such as high blood pressure, chronic headaches, diabetes or heart attack. On the other hand, if we "keep cool" under stress, we may avoid all the above problems and be much happier persons.

The skills to deal with stress can be learned quite easily. Biofeedback is a form of self-awareness training whose goal is to help you become more in control of your emotions and body functions. With the assistance of our trained nurse or biofeedback technician you will learn how to lower your heart rate and blood pressure, improve your circulation, "cool down" nervous perspiration and thoroughly loosen your muscles. Relaxation exercises will be demonstrated which you can practice at home to help you achieve these goals. With continued practice and with the opportunity to learn from watching your responses, you can achieve a level of self-control and peace of mind you may not have thought possible. This technique can then be called upon in prayer or to help provide support in a variety of everyday stressful situations, e.g., when in a traffic jam. CES combined with biofeedback is even more effective.

Biofeedback training has already proven very helpful in treating many conditions including high blood pressure, heart disease, asthma, headaches (migraine and tension), certain forms of poor circulation (Raynaud's phenomenon), impotence, peptic ulcer, irritable bowel and muscle spasms. In addition, it is an essential aid in achieving smoking cessation and modifying chronic anxiety states. CES combined with biofeedback is even more effective to reduce anxiety, hostility, and internal anger which contributes to heart disease.

Relaxation usually generalizes to the rest of the body. Our ability to control certain relaxation techniques in circulation, in the hands or the pulse, can generalize to the whole system. Most of all, relaxation techniques that focus on brain wave training have the widest benefits because the nervous system and the brain are involved with more aspects of body functions than any other body system. Biofeedback has been useful in the following disorders: migraine headache, gastrointestinal and muscular disorders, anxiety, epilepsy and cerebral palsy.

Biofeedback is a tool for releasing potential, similar to prayer and meditation, except that it makes use of medical technology to give an individual more feedback. Brain wave training is particularly useful because the brain has no sensory processes by which it can detect its own brain wave activity. Your hands may feel cold, but you may not know that you are in the theta wave rather than the alpha wave. You can get a sense of the brain's control through the technique of biofeedback. It is a dreamlike state and is particularly useful for increasing imagery. One of the goals of biofeedback training is to increase the normal alpha frequency, which normally decreases with age, and enable you to have the flexibility to go into the fringe of consciousness and theta states. Ultimately, theta is easier to suppress under the control of the conscious individual and alpha frequency can be increased.

This is the way in which the sounds are made audible. The lower limit of hearing is 25 hertz, but the average alpha frequency is 10 hertz, which is inaudible without amplification. By multiplying it by 200, the average alpha feedback tone goes to 2,000 hertz, which lies within the range of the human hearing spectrum and generates a series of musical tones which can sound like flute music. Theta feedback sounds more like an oboe. Imagery can help induce these kinds of states. Visualization and imagery may be the best way of programming the body and reaching the body's immune system. In fact, there have been some studies suggesting visualization as an aid to cancer, immune disorder recovery and the reversal of stress that leads to heart disease.

In Christian mysticism that path has been called Jacob's ladder. In China the path is called Tao. In Sanskrit the path is called Antakarana. Both Christians and Jews have been called the people of God's path (Book of Acts and Isaiah 35). Although the path to biofeedback is in its early development, the goal ultimately is to fulfill what is said in Deuteronomy 6, which is a combination of prayer and meditation with the connection between mind and body through the CES device which is a modern phylactery for anxiety and stress. The power of biofeedback lies in its effect on stress. Every individual facing a disease has a triple stress: the stress that predated the disease and which was a factor leading to its onset; the stress of having the disease with all its threats to self-image, identity, and personal security; and the stress of the treatment—painful, frightening and depleting. Biofeedback can lead to quiet emotions, and quiet emotions can promote a quite body and inner peace. Self-regulation is at the core, but really regulation by the higher power is ultimately what is accomplished in biofeedback. Let go, let God, is what is accomplished in the biofeedback session: getting on the PATH.

In epilepsy, another potential rhythm for treating biofeed-back is 12 to 14 hertz, or mu rhythm, also recorded from the rolandic cortex. Some studies have suggested that a mu rhythm is often described as an abnormal rhythm because of its appearance. Reverie is designated as 7 to 9 hertz and can also help reduce seizure frequency. Many musculoskeletal problems have been amenable to biofeedback treatment, including:

Prolonged immobilization
Myositis ossificans
Joint repair
Elevated activity following back strain
Frozen shoulder
Muscle tendon transfer
Substitution movements
Muscle strengthening and relaxation
Whiplash
Muscle shortening
Asymmetry and homologous trunk or back muscles

Biofeedback can also be used for neuromuscular reeducation, stretch reflex and tactile stimulation, among other activities.

The idea behind biofeedback training is to use sensitive detectors to tell you what is happening inside your own body so you can have a better sense of changes occurring in your body which are associated with various emotions. This will ultimately give you a sense of assisted relaxation, assisted prayer and assisted meditation.

In human history, unconscious, involuntary processes for-mally sent feedback signals only to the hypothalamus. We can now give feedback signals to the cortex. Closing the biocyber-netic loop means bridging the normal gap between conscious and unconscious and voluntary and involuntary processes. It is accomplishing voluntary self-regulation through imagination and visualization. There are also many dimensions used in biofeedback which include not only regular biofeedback techniques, but also verbal and medical biofeedback techniques as well; such as measuring urinary cotinine levels, salivary cyanide, expired carbon monoxide, etc. in smokers. With biofeedback, people can learn to recognize essential stress cues that they might not normally recognize.

BASIC RULES FOR ESTABLISHING GOOD BIOFEEDBACK

Biofeedback attempts to connect the mind to the body. Some basic work between temperature, heart training, EMG, or smooth muscle training, such as pelvic, bladder, or bowel control, may be useful. Attention deficit disorders and memory/concentration problems use the beta-theta approach, and relaxation uses the alpha-theta approach. Usually 6 skin temperature training sessions are done to maintain digit skin temperature of 95 degrees for 10 minutes.

Alpha feedback training can be done using the 01 monopolar placement, OZ or P2 (even the T3 electrode can be placed on the basis of the BEAM abnormality), with auditory feedback on alpha when alpha percent is greater than 40 percent. When alpha reaches 50 percent, theta training can replace alpha. When theta percent reaches 50 percent, biofeedback for both alpha and theta feedback can be done with a different bell for each. For certain kinds of disorganization and cloudy consciousness, beta training is not done until relaxation is learned.

Biofeedback is sometimes a very confusing topic. Biofeedback refers to the use of electronic medical devices to give more auditory, verbal and visual information back to the body about how it is working. For example, during biofeedback, when one tries to relax one's muscles, one can hear a sound telling the degree of relaxation. Or if one aims to slow one's pulse, one can hear or see one's pulse more easily than by just feeling the pulse. By hearing the pulse; it is easier to try to manipulate it with one's conscious control. This is also done with temperature control. When people are nervous, their hands might get colder or sweaty and warmer. With biofeedback we learn to control our vascular and nervous system.

During biofeedback, by giving auditory and/or visual signals, individuals are able to better direct their conscious thoughts and thus control what would normally be outside their control. Everyday our nervous systems interact with our bodies. In Peace and/or in Christ, in healthiness and Godliness, both our minds and our bodies are one; they are the temples of the Holy Spirit. In many illnesses, this connection is severed.

For many individuals the consequence of anxiety is a decreased immune system, manifested by increased colds and disease. They may also experience anxiety in one or some of these forms:

Palpitations	Difficulty swallowing
Sweaty hands or cold hands	Diarrhea
Shortness of breath	Constipation
Light-headedness	Frequent urination
Headache	Numbness in the hands and toes
Eye Strain	Acne

There are vital ways in which the mind or brain's chemistry affects the body's health. This is the connection that we are trying to make for people with biofeedback. Helping individuals to understand this connection between the mind and the body and how their emotions impact their temperature, vascular system, pulse rate, bowel and bladder habits is the first step.

THE SPIRITUAL DIMENSION

Biofeedback has been used by proponents of the New Age movement to access what is known as lower consciousness, and what is sometimes thought of as demonic, unconscious, psychic or channeling processes. Biofeedback can now be used to access higher consciousness by altering the drowsiness states of certain individuals who have abnormal brain chemistry or abnormal neurological states on brain mapping, such as a low P300 wave (a positive brain wave which occurs at about ⅓ of a second). These individuals can learn brain exercises in order to move from the theta state or drowsiness state to a more alert, creative mind frame in the alpha state. These individuals can also reduce anxiety and all its manifestations, which include ulcers, palpitations, smoking, overeating, irritability, anger, etc., in both their emotional and physical components.

Biofeedback can easily become a Biblical or meditative experience depending on patient choice. For example:

1. The use of imagery in biofeedback can be selected from prophetic images: God and His chariot (Ezekiel); the scroll extended from heaven to earth (Revelation); the talking donkey (Numbers); turning water into wine (John); clock turning backwards (Chronicles); sun standing still (Joshua); walking on water (Gospels); dead coming back to life (Revelation). God provides prophetic imagery in the Bible because of its relaxing, beneficial effect on the brain. By using prophetic imagery in the context of biofeedback, one can maximize the healing effect of imagery on the brain's physical nervous system.

2. The use of a form of biofeedback which emphasizes meditative quiet. The Biblical principle here is "Be still and know that the Lord is God." This principle applies to both meditation and good concentration. There is a time during which a person must be still in order to experience his/her

connection to a higher power (for example, the Lord God Jesus Christ—LGJC/Yahweh), however one may know it.

3. The use of an aspect of biofeedback which works on repetitive thought processing and cognitive drilling. This is equivalent to repetitive, incessant or contemplative prayer. Various prayers can be used during the biofeedback process as an attempt to increase the alpha-theta transition state, a state in which we can dream and see visions, in an attempt to gain greater emotional and intellectual flexibility.

4. Many individuals want to use biofeedback to increase their alpha waves because the alpha state is more creative. There is no greater source of creativity than being in touch with the Creator or Higher Power Himself.

5. Use of still another form of biofeedback—relaxation and experiencing the Sabbath peace (which surpasses all understanding); evidence suggests that this is an important part of total holiness. The practice of biofeedback can improve one's ability to willfully relax and therefore makes it easier to "turn off" one day per week in a society that never turns off and never stops. Relaxation training, therefore, is an important part of the Biblical path.

6. Biofeedback can be used to help an individual learn to control the vascular and nervous system in his/her body. In God there is no pain, no death, no sorrow. Pain control is achieved when one is able to shut off certain neural circuits as pain's pathways. This becomes a Biblical tool for greater self-control which is a gift of God's Holy Spirit—who teaches a reality far greater than a higher power, greater and more important than any power known in this world.

7. Biofeedback has also been used to control blood pressure. The Biblical principle here is that the brain controls the body as the heavens controls the earth; therefore, the heart

and pulse rate and other bodily functions can be controlled by the brain. We need to look at biofeedback as a way of extending the heavenly and spiritual control of the brain into the body. If the spirit of God controls one's brain, one will have better total health overall. When the brain truly has control, it can control various bodily functions such as acidity in the stomach, diarrhea, palpitations, etc. What we try to accomplish with biofeedback is to break the circuitry if the brain has irregular rhythms, before they cause disease. We combine biofeedback with Cranial Electrical Stimulation to maximize effectiveness.

8. Everyone doing the biofeedback in a prayerful spirit is actually building up his/her immune system.

9. Scientists claim that by using biofeedback one can gain answers to one's problems from one's inner self. Believers in God know that the Kingdom of God is within them— the source of all truth. This connection to God, or Higher Consciousness, can be achieved by increasing the alpha state, which is the goal of biofeedback.

God has given us the spirit of self-control and any technique that helps us master self-control is moving us along the path toward total holiness. By reading and meditating on the Word in conjunction with special biofeedback techniques, one can reach a higher state of consciousness/Godliness.

BIOFEEDBACK AND IMAGERY

Biofeedback is a useful way to exercise the brain. It can be used to augment alpha and theta brain waves, which can help individuals with headaches, irritable bowel syndrome, stomach problems, palpitations, and other brain chemically mediated stress conditions. To help the doctor develop the best images to use during the biofeedback training system, three or four images of the following subjects should be written down: images of peace related to family, images of peace related to the world, images of peace related to finances, images of peace related to self, images of peace related to work, images of peace related to the community or society. These images should be numbered in order of importance.

BIOFEEDBACK AND MEDITATION

With biofeedback, many people ultimately come in touch with the inner path of their life. In the West, it is called the source, talent and strength of each person, the source of their creativity, sometimes called the ego, the transpersonal spiritual self of every person. This ego is distinct from the ego of psychology and psychiatry—it is an extension of the personality and frequently called the soul. The personality is sometimes defined as the sum total of our physical, emotional, mental, and stereotypical characteristics, limited by heredity, conditioning, culture, experience, and education. It is an ego often thought to be the immortal self which transcends the personality, opens the door to the genuinely creative, unpredictable, undeduced solution of the body, emotions, and mind. In China, this source of the soul is called the Tao, or the path. In Zen it is called true self. In India it is called true self or Jiva. The path concept is common both in China and in Christianity and Judaism. In the Book of Acts, early Christians were called to be on the path. Derech HaShem, or the path to God, has been the great tradition in Judaism.

Biofeedback shows us that there is control over the body and the soul or self. Even single muscle cells can be controlled by volition. There can be autogenic training of the bladder, muscles. Our bodies are equipped with regulating mechanisms that work automatically. Thank God we don't have to think and say, "Heart, start beating," nor do we have to remind our lungs to breathe. But we do impact these automatic mechanisms when we catch our breath after being startled, when we blush due to embarrassment, or when our mouths water when we smell food. It is important to have some sense that your body is impacted by your mind, and biofeedback helps individuals who have numerous mind-body connection problems, such as allergies and immune system disorders. The brain regulates all these systems, such as the bowel and the bladder; and what biofeedback can do is help reconnect the brain's control of these areas.

BIOFEEDBACK TECHNIQUES AT PATH

One of the biofeedback techniques at PATH is autogenic training of the heart. Patients are taught to hear their heart rate: their heartbeat is put on a loud speaker and they try to relax and slow down their heart rate. They use the beat as an indication of their progress. They can do this with their hand, electrodes or with a Doppler device. Cardiac patients have been able to study the behavior of their hearts by watching and/or hearing their EKG signals. In some cases patients can reduce the frequency of their PVC's which can be induced by anxiety. PVCs or preventricular contractions are the most common irregular heartbeat.

Diseases that occur without our realizing it, like Raynaud's and poor circulation, frequently occur with anxiety. Many individuals can learn to control their hand temperature ten to twenty degrees, which can make it possible to overcome this problem. There is a king cell or primary neuronucleus in the primary subcortical structures that can help control this. Mind-body duality as a healing concept can be achieved through biofeedback before the brain makes the body critically sick; for example, when the irritable bowel syndrome of anxiety progresses to diverticulosis because of the combination of poor food choices and stress.

BIOFEEDBACK AND STRESS

Biofeedback can help numerous conditions which are a result of stress, such as psychiatric conditions, anxiety, depression, substance abuse disorders, sleep disorders, learning disabilities, hyperactivity, tinnitus, agoraphobia, and neurological conditions such as temporal lobe epilepsy and manic-depression. Biofeedback can also help allergic conditions such as asthma by reducing reactivity, as well as helping immune disorders and skin disorders. Other conditions in which stress is probably the major contributor are PMS (premenstrual syndome), colitis, Raynaud's syndrome (cold extremities), palpitations, and the cardiovascular disorders such as high blood pressure. Biofeedback techniques also can help a person learn to avoid stress.

Chelation Therapy— Washing the Inner Heart: Another Critical Adjunct to Reversal of Cardiovascular Disease

The word chelation is derived from the Greek word "chel," meaning "to claw." Chelation is a common reaction in both the biological and chemical world. The chelation reaction is used by both organic and inorganic chemists. EDTA, ethylene diamine tetra acetic acid (an amino acid), was first synthesized by Franz Munz, a German chemist, for use in textile and fabric production. Chelation therapy, in conjunction with sodium citrate, was first used in medicine for lead poisoning.

Over the last several decades, the medical application of chelation therapy has continued to grow, although some opposition has grown as well. Some of the early studies using EDTA have found it removes heavy metals from the body, especially calcium. This characteristic was severely criticized by orthodox medicine. Orthodox physicians pointed out that chelation robs the body of vitamins, mainly B6, and may even chelate an abundance of calcium from the bones and teeth. Newer applications of this therapy have been accompanied by a vitamin regimen designed to replace whatever is lost.

The decalcification of teeth or bones with chelation therapy cannot occur under these conditions. Protocols instituted by the new American Board of Chelation Therapy have reduced side effects to virtually zero.

Oral EDTA was used at first, but this actually increased lead and heavy metal absorption from the lower intestines. Today, this method of delivery is strongly discouraged. Early studies also tended to encourage the infusion of too high an EDTA concentration too quickly. This caused problems in patients, especially those on cardiac drugs. Now, over 3 million chelation treatments have been given to over 300,000 patients. Lead, cadmium, arsenic, aluminum, and excess iron pour out of the "rusting," aged patient who undergoes chelation. It usually results in an overall, fantastic benefit of general increased well-being and health.

EDTA, the chelating agent, donates an electron to the ligand, which is usually calcium or another metal. Once bound, this complex can be eliminated through the urine. Chelation therapy has been used for arteriosclerosis, lead or other heavy metal intoxification, memory loss, senility, Alzheimer's disease, diabetic gangrene, impaired vision, kidney stones, high blood pressure, and a host of other maladies. In one case, a 54-year-old chiropractor had been saved from a leg amputation for diabetic gangrene by chelation therapy. Another doctor used chelation to lower his cholesterol (which it did), and noticed a great improvement in his memory. Certain eye diseases, for example, macular degeneration where circulation is diminished, are greatly helped by EDTA chelation therapy due to its cleansing effect on the blood vessels.

Although it has had numerous applications, perhaps the most widely used one is for treatment of cardiovascular disease, including high blood pressure and arteriosclerosis. EDTA is a nonspecific chelator, although it focuses on calcium since this is in abundance. By doing this, EDTA stabilizes intracellular membranes of the cells of the arteries. In addition, it helps to correct enzyme inhibition which is concomitant with the advancing of the disease. It also assists in stabilizing the electric charge of platelets, and thus reduces platelet leukocyte interaction leading to a reduction in unnecessary clotting. It can act as a calcium channel blocker and thus lower unnecessary arterial vasoconstrictions. The process of calcification is intimately associated with sclerotic hardening, and this can be reversed by EDTA chelation.

While the potential benefits of chelation therapy are currently unobtainable anywhere in orthodox medicine, it can save countless cardiovascular patients from the horrors of bypass surgery and other high-risk, low-success-rate techniques. Chelation therapy is possibly a great overall antioxidant technique.

Exercise

There are so many benefits to exercise—you can live longer, be healthier, and reduce triglyceride and cholesterol levels. There can be problems with long-term exercise, e.g., marathon running, in that it can decrease fertility and sex drive. Many studies show that exercise reduces hypertension, which is (next to obesity) the best predictor of reduced lifespan.

Sedentary people can have shriveled up hearts; they actually have shrinking heart muscle. Inadequate exercise can predict that a person will not live as long as the person that does exercise because exercise can lower blood pressure from 10 to 15 points. Walking is an exceptionally good form of exercise, whereas long-distance running depletes zinc, chromium, and magnesium. (Depletion of magnesium can cause instant death.) Marathon running can reduce the male sex drive as well as cause anemia. Also common in marathon runners are tibial fractures and pelvic stress fractures.

Moderate exercise is a healthful activity in that it has many benefits. It can reduce the chance that a woman will develop osteoporosis. Weight-lifting and aerobic exercise seem to reduce triglycerides. Exercise lowers the fat in the blood, thus reducing the risk of heart disease. Exercise also increases metabolic rate, thus reducing weight. Exercise is particularly useful in high-calorie diets.

An athlete in training will experience: a loss of choline, vitamin B6, riboflavin, vitamin C (reduces lung stress), as well as the loss in sweat of zinc and chromium. High complex carbohydrate diets are highly recommended for endurance training. Yet, sugar or refined carbohydrates can cause a loss of energy during an athletic performance.

Some preparation tips for exercise are: 1) eat at least 3 to 4 hours before a major athletic event; 2) eat complex carbohydrates (whole grains, brown rice, whole-wheat toast); 3) limit protein intake (the more protein you eat, the more you urinate); 4) eliminate gassy foods and sugar (a quick sugar high stimulates insulin secretion which can result in hypoglycemic episodes, thus, draining energy); 5) drink plenty of water; and 6) avoid caffeine and alcohol.

It's important to exercise consistently and moderately. The need for B vitamins, zinc, chromium, carotene, choline, potassium, and magnesium increases with strenuous exercise. Heavy sweating can result in depletion of potassium or magnesium levels and can create heart rhythm problems. Additionally, long-distance runners may have less breast cancer because of a reduction in sex hormones, i.e., testosterone and estrogen.

Severe exercise can increase endorphins (natural pain killers). A runner's high comes from the release of natural pain relievers, endorphins. Marathon running is like a short-term antidepressant. Yet, the overall effects of extreme exercise (marathon training) are not beneficial. In contrast, swimming is excellent for osteoporosis and arthritis.

HOW MUCH EXERCISE SHOULD I DO?

The more active a person is, the stronger his bones will be. Becoming more active is a gradual process. You can begin by working more physical activity into your everyday routine. Make a point to walk more during your day and to take the stairs instead of the elevator or escalator.

If you are presently engaging in aerobic, weight-bearing exercise which is of moderate intensity (e.g., aerobic dancing, slow jogging or brisk walking), you should aim to participate in this activity a minimum of three days a week for 20 to 30 minutes. This level of activity is adequate for preventing the development of osteoporosis. You also may wish to increase the level of routine activity that you do by increasing the amount of walking you do. You may also wish to add some exercise to increase strength in your arms, shoulders, chest and back.

If you are not presently exercising regularly, consider beginning a program of regular walking. Walking is generally the recommended exercise for preventing and treating osteoporosis since it is a safe, effective exercise that everyone can do.

HOW MUCH WALKING SHOULD I DO?

The amount of exercise you should do depends on several factors including your age, health, and physical condition. The intensity of the exercise will also affect how often you exercise. Mild exercise, such as walking at a comfortable pace, can be done daily. Thirty minutes of walking a day is believed to be enough exercise to stimulate bones and keep them strong and healthy. Moderate exercise, such as brisk walking, can be done three to five days a week, for 20 to 30 minutes. If you are not used to exercising regularly, or if you have any medical or orthopedic problems, you will need to gradually work up to this level of exercise. Begin slowly and progress gradually. Set small goals for exercise each week. For example, you may wish to begin with 10 to 15 minutes of walking, three days per week. As you feel stronger, gradually increase the amount of exercise you do. Listen to your body and don't push yourself.

EXERCISE BENEFITS

Exercise releases neuromuscular hormones into the brain, and this has a beneficial effect on depression, anxiety, insomnia, etc. Exercise may even improve nutrient absorption and utilization. Exercise has tremendous psychological and physical health benefits.

Leg Cramps

Leg cramps are usually of two types: 1) those that occur during the day due to exercise, and 2) those that occur at night. Daytime leg cramps due to strenuous exercise (or even walking) are usually a sign of vascular insufficiency. There are numerous nutrients that have been suggested to be helpful, e.g., fish oil (Mega-EPA), vitamin E, and garlic, which are antiplatelet, aspirin-like drugs that thin the blood. Niacin may also be useful because of its vasodilating effect (like the drug Vasodilan and others). Potassium must also be considered, because potassium deficiency can cause muscle spasm. Calcium and magnesium can also decrease daytime cramping. Persantine, which reduces the stickiness of red cells, can also be used.

Night cramps are often precipitated by stretching or extending legs during rest or light sleep. Walking sometimes brings relief. Others claim that raising the foot of the bed by nine inches is also helpful. Some drugs can cause nocturnal cramps, which disappear after drug withdrawal. Quinine, on the other hand, is sometimes helpful in low dosages because it is a mild muscle relaxant and blood thinner. Excessive use of quinine (an herbal) can cause tinnitus, nausea and headache, and it should not be used during pregnancy. We try to stick to the use of vitamin E, calcium, magnesium, potassium, niacin, fish oil and diet to treat both day and night cramps.

Nutrients to Prevent Heart Attacks

Niacin reduces cholesterol and probably reduces the risk of heart attacks. At least one gram daily is needed to lower cholesterol and raise HDL. Because niacin in doses of that size opens (dilates) blood vessels, flushing occurs. Patients should start at doses of 100 mg twice a day with meals, doubling the dose every three days. If the flush is too great at any dose, the next dose should be cut by ½ or ¼. The flush effect can be reduced by aspirin. A new zero-flush brand allows starting doses to begin at 800 mg with rapid increase to 2 to 3 grams.

Hard water (high calcium and magnesium) protects against heart disease, while soft water with too much copper from the pipes promotes heart disease. Zinc and vitamin C can be used to reduce heavy metal levels, especially copper, lead and cadmium. Magnesium is in hard water and is a useful therapy in various arrhythmias and when deficient can produce arrhythmia and increase the size of the heart attack. The type A personality (overachiever) tends to lose their magnesium more easily. Twenty percent of patients admitted to intensive care units show decreases in magnesium. Magnesium is nature's physiologic calcium channel blocker, similar in its effects to the use of such drugs as Verapamil and Diltiazem. Magnesium, particularly as an oxide, is useful in the treatment of hypertension. Diuretics deplete potassium, magnesium and zinc as well as other electrolytes significantly.

A recent study of fish consumption (in the *New England Journal of Medicine*) suggested that as little as one or two dishes per week may be of preventative value. Fish oil, like niacin and garlic, can raise HDL (the good cholesterol). Fish oil anticoagulates the blood as does aspirin.

Several other nutrients have been found to be deficient in patients with coronary artery disease. Low plasma chromium is found in coronary artery and other heart disease patients.

Serum selenium has been found to be significantly reduced in patients with acute myocardial infarction. Cardiomyopathy has been associated with vitamin E deficiency. Decreases in serum linoleic acid (polyunsaturated oil) have been implemented in predisposing individuals to reinfarction. Antioxidants have a positive role in patients with coronary artery disease, probably reducing the risk of death. Vitamin B6 has important diuretic properties and is essential to the lowering of blood pressure.

Other dietary suggestions are to follow a high-vegetable, low-fat, reduced-meat diet, and to avoid all saturated fats and hydrogenated oils. It is advisable to eat large amounts of whole grains, use polyunsaturated oil (e.g., safflower or sunflower oil) liberally on salads, and consume high pectin fruits (apples, bananas).

Drugs for Many Purposes

Doctors use medications in many different ways. For example, aspirin, which is listed as an antipyretic (pyretic means fever), is a fever drug, yet we use it for thinning the blood for heart disease, for headache (ordinary), migraine, arthritis, pain, etc. Advil, which was originally designed for fever, can be used for dysmenorrhea or even PMS. Antiseizure drugs, like Tegretol, can be used not only for seizure, but also for brain dysrhythmia, manic depression, depression, anxiety, and biochemical imbalance. Mellaril, which is listed as an antipsychotic, can be used for depression, melancholia, biochemical imbalance, and dopamine metabolic control. Antidepressants such as Prozac can be used for weight loss, appetite reduction, treatment of lower back pain, peptic ulcer disease, fibrositis, headache, peripheral neuropathy, rheumatoid disease, and irritable colon. All so-called antidepressants can be used for medical problems. In fact, 25 percent or more of all prescriptions of antidepressants are for nonpsychiatric disorders. Benzodiazepines, like Klonopin, can be used for anxiety but also seizure disorder, temporal lobe disorder, and biochemical imbalance.

Most brain chemical treatments have multiple uses, and no patient should be confused by the class of the drug because its classification does not tell its multiple uses. The antianginal drug Procardia is used for hypertension, and the antihypertensive drug Clonidine is used for appetite suppression, mania and drug withdrawal from cigarettes, methadone and heroin. As much as 30 to 60 percent of all prescribing of drugs by physicians is for something outside the original purpose for which the drug was designed. This is also true of nutrients—many nutrients have multiple purposes. Magnesium can help with angina and hypertension but also work as a laxative. Methionine can work for arthritis and allergies and work as an antihistamine. Other antihistamines like Benadryl can be used for insomnia or decongestion or even allergic reaction. In sum, most substances can't be classified as limited to treating one or a limited number of diseases.

SYMPTOMS AND
SIDE EFFECTS OF MEDICATIONS

Indigestion	Palpitations
Dizziness	Constipation or diarrhea
Fatigue	Numbness or pain in the nerves
Headache	Breathing difficulty
Impotence	Hair loss
Depression	Anxiety

Sexual Brain Health and Increasing the Sex Drive

Integral to having a healthy brain is the presence of a healthy sex drive. It is no surprise that antidepressants like Welbutrin and Nardil can impact sexual health in either a negative or positive manner. Usually Welbutrin, tyrosine, DL-phenylalanine and zinc increase sex drive. For some individuals—both men and women—Yocon (or yohimbine chloride, another adrenaline-producing herb) can be a tremendous sex stimulant and can be taken in doses as high as 40 mg per day safely (watch high blood pressure). Sex is a barometer of brain health and brain neurotransmitter function. Frequently, sex can be affected by numerous diseases which are the result of bad habits, such as diabetes due to sugar and carbohydrate addiction, and vascular disease due to smoking. These bad habits (and therefore the disease) are avoidable if the brain rhythm is correct and addiction does not set in. Nutrients and medicine can overcome the damaging effect of drugs in sexual function.

Infertility and Impotence

Much has been said about sex, nutrition and fertility, but very little is known. The role of zinc, calcium, carnitine and arginine in sperm function has suggested possible roles for these nutrients in combating infertility. A drug that inhibits phenylalanine metabolism can cause male infertility since it is possible that phenylalanine may promote fertility and sex drive. A high-fat and protein diet also may promote fertility, since fat is converted to sex hormones.

Most infertility we see is due to marijuana abuse or occupational chemical exposure. Caffeine and nicotine may also have a negative effect on sperm.

An evaluation of various nutrients is important. A conventional endocrinology workup is essential for all cases of infertility. Infertility in women is easier to solve with the use of various hormones (e.g., Pergamol, LHRH (Lutenizing Hormone Releasing Hormone), Clomid) than infertility in men.

Impotence in men is a common problem. Nutrients that increase circulation, e.g., niacin, EPA, vitamin E, have been suggested as useful. A drug, Yohimex (Yocon), increases catecholamines and sex drive, as may the amino acids tyrosine, phenylalanine and methionine (methionine increases absorption). Vitamin E therapy has been used to treat the unusual Peyronie's disease (fibrous disease of the penis).

High doses of Yocon, up to 40 mg a day, can drastically increase sex drive but can raise blood pressure. Most impotence problems that will not respond to nutrients and yohimbine (Yocon) have an organic basis and require an external blood evaluation for hormone imbalance and diseases like diabetes and arteriosclerosis, which are often causes of impotence. Treatment of the underlying problem will contribute to cardiovascular health.

Male Menopause (Andropause)

Male menopause occurs in men over time. It probably begins anywhere from age 30 to 50, when men start losing DHEA (dehydroepoendostrione) as well as levels of testosterone, free and total, and growth hormone diminishes and insulin increases. This is similar to what happens with women where their ovaries and adrenal glands start to deteriorate and get fewer signals from the hypothalamus and the aging/dying cycle begins. Both men and women can start replacing DHEA at early stages in their lives and may eventually be able to do low-dose growth hormone replacement. Such replacements will result in a slowing of the aging process.

New studies again highlight how common male menopause is. Men over 50 can have tremendous improvement with injections of male hormone. They may experience improvement in strength, balance, red blood cell count, lowering cholesterol and reduction of angina, according to a study by Dr. Shi of St. Louis University School of Medicine, presented at the American Geriatric Society.

Weekly testosterone shots are extremely successful. Men on these hormone shots, natural testosterone injection, also available in pill form, have significantly larger muscles, better strength and are significantly stronger than those individuals given placebo, as well as lower cholesterol.

A similar study done by Dr. Phillips at Roosevelt/St. Luke's Hospital in Manhattan showed that men have reduced heart attack risk when taking testosterone. He also confirms safety and effectiveness. There was no increase in prostate problems identified.

The amount of testosterone correlated with high-density lipoproteins which protect against arteriosclerosis. It has been suggested that taking saw palmetto herb or zinc with testosterone will diminish the potential risk, if any, of prostate enlargement.

Patients are less likely to develop angina when taking the testosterone. Incidents of heart attacks increase as testosterone goes down. Better regulation of blood sugar may occur with men who take testosterone supplements. Men with angina have lower levels of testosterone.

Several other studies have also shown that the administration of testosterone results in decreased risks of heart attacks. The correlation of low testosterone and coronary artery disease is now highly significant and relatively well-established.

Adrenopause and DHEA

More research has been done on adrenopause as we now start to better understand what dying is. Dying is the death of various glands, particularly those that are distant from the brain which are the source of life such as the testicles, ovaries, adrenal gland, thyroid and the pancreas, which produces growth hormone.

A paper presented at the American Psychiatric Association (subdivision Biological Psychiatry) submitted by Dr. Russe at the University of California at San Francisco showed that DHEA is low in people with declining memory and aging.

Preliminary data showed that cognitively impaired individuals have lower levels of this hormone and that therapeutic trials were recommended.

These substances, DHEA and DHEAS (the sulphated form), are both low in individuals with aging memory problems as well as in individuals with depression. Fifty mg per day in individuals over 50 has remarkable effects on well-being.

Low DHEA, like low thyroid, is a marker of aging and dying.

DHEA DEFICIENCY MAY ALSO CONTROL BLOOD PRESSURE AND HEART DISEASE

New studies show that the higher the concentration of DHEA, the less likely the man will have impotence. A study by Robert F. McGivern of Harbor UCLA Medical Center in the January 1990 issue of *Teratology* suggested that post-magnetic fields, low frequency, might result in demasculinization and that electromagnetic fields (EMF) may be another environmental feminizer which can be estrogenically producing cancer for women and affecting male health.

A study reviewed in the January 8, 1994, issue of *Science News* showed that 39 percent of men with heart disease and 15 percent of men with hypertension had impotence. The most significant factor was not testosterone but DHEA. We are one of the first clinics to do DHEA blood testing on all men between 50 and 70, and we have been able to identify that low levels of this natural adrenal hormone result in a variety of problems, such as sexual dysfunction, premature aging, inability to handle stress. Essentially this is a state called adrenopause.

DHEA—TREATMENT FOR OBESITY

DHEA is a steroid hormone produced by the adrenal glands. DHEA is the most abundant steroid in the human bloodstream. Research has suggested that it may have significant antiobesity, anticancer and anti-aging effects. DHEA blood levels drop naturally as people age. Additionally, DHEA, like estrogen and progesterone, may have an important role in cognitive enhancement.

DHEA protects brain cells from Alzheimer's disease and other degenerative conditions. Nerve degeneration may occur readily under low DHEA conditions. Brain tissues naturally contain 6.5 times more DHEA than is found in other tissues. By adding low concentrations of DHEA to nerve cell tissue cultures, we can increase the number of neurons, their ability to establish contacts and their differentiation. DHEA may also enhance long-term memory in mice. Perhaps it plays a similar role in human brain function. Low levels in obesity are common as are high insulin levels, and low growth hormone levels. DHEA may be an alternative for estrogen intolerant individuals.

DHEA is now being administered to Alzheimer's patients in scientific studies. People with Alzheimer's may have 48 percent less DHEA than matched controls of the same age. DHEA may be low in other degenerative diseases, e.g., diabetes, Parkinson's, etc. DHEA deficiency probably should be treated in most cases.

A prescription is required. In order to obtain DHEA and other hormones, a written prescription from an M.D. or D.O. is required.

Estrogen:
Natural Hormones for Lowering Blood Pressure and Stabilizing Heart Disease

PATH Medical continues to treat with natural hormones. These treatments are beneficial for male menopause and women who are looking for a non-period, low-side effect natural estrogen. Evidence is now suggesting that Estriol, another form of natural estrogen which is high during pregnancy, will actually prevent breast cancer and may need to replace Estradiol and Estrone. Articles by Dr. Follingstad in 1978 and Dr. Lemon in 1966 were generally ignored, but new suggestions by Dr. Julian Whitaker and Dr. Jonathan Wright suggest that this might be an alternative way of supplementing estrogen. We are looking into it and trying to evaluate the data, but it certainly may be worth a try in many women. The ideal hormone replacement would be a combination of Estriol, Estradiol, progesterone and natural testosterone. This can lower blood pressure, reverse or stabilize heart disease. All natural hormone therapies have been shown to positively impact heart disease; the degree of reversal and stabilization depends on each patient. It depends on each patient's deficiencies, supplement level and biochemical individuality.

Melatonin: A Modified Amino Acid

Melatonin is a hormone produced by the brain's pineal gland, a light-sensitive gland that is sometimes referred to as our third eye. Melatonin is relatively benign in nature and low in toxicity. Some people think it shrinks tumors when taken in high doses. Unfortunately it is very difficult to obtain. Twenty and 30 mg pills are available by prescription; in some cases as much as 80 to 250 mg have been used to help individuals sleep and to regulate the hormonal cycle. Melatonin is now available in pure form and should not be purchased in any other form. It may help lower blood pressure in that it can relax, calm, reduce stress and help improve sleep. It also may relieve heart cancer and decrease other cancer risks and development.

Melatonin is derived from the amino acid tryptophan by the action of two enzymes in the pineal gland. Dietary tryptophan is converted in the body to serotonin. Serotonin is then

converted to melatonin by the enzymes N-aceytl-transferase
(NAT) and Hydroxy-indol-o-methyl transferase (HIOMT). In
essence, melatonin is a modified amino acid whose rate limiting step is NAT.

Human production of melatonin was thought to be independent of external light because melatonin levels did not
increase in response to room light.

By 1980, it was shown that substantially brighter light, 2,500
lux or five times the usual intensity of room light, was necessary to inhibit human melatonin production. Subsequent studies show that daily melatonin production could be shifted by
timing bright light stimulus. Bright light scheduled in the
morning advanced the melatonin rhythm, shifted the onset to
an earlier time (wake up early, go to bed early). Bright light
scheduled in the evening delayed it, so people stayed up later.
We believe that the melatonin cycle best reflects the phase
of internal circadian pacemaker. No surprise, the pineal gland
was thought to be the seat of the soul (by René Descartes);
at least it's the seat of the circadian rhythms!

Production of melatonin from the pineal glands is stimu-
lated by sympathetic neuro output from other super chias-
matic nuclei. Melatonin production begins in the evening,
sometimes after dusk, somewhere around 8:00 pm and it
peaks at about 12:00 and has another peak at about 4 a.m.,
and finally should be gone by 6 a.m. Morning melatonin levels
are low daytime concentrations, although people differ at
onset. Each individual variability is minimal.

Melatonin production is a useful marker for understanding
the entire circadian rhythm pacemaking. If subjects are kept
in dim light 30 to 50 lux, they avoid suppression of melatonin
production. And bright white light can be used to shift cycles.
If you take the melatonin around 8 at night you are getting
a boost to your melatonin production. You are more likely
to fall asleep and get into a deeper sleep. If you take it too
late, you might find yourself waking up in the morning as if
you are sleeping (the sleep hormone effect) but feeling as if

it was four in the morning physically. So you must be careful with melatonin so that you don't get yourself into too deep a sleep because what it does is it puts your whole body to sleep. It can shift your entire sleep phase. So if you arrive on a jet lag and it's 2 A.M. and you want to get to your destination time (say, California time, if you live in New York) you can start taking it right away at 8 P.M. at your destination time, or you can take it earlier on your plane ride and put yourself to sleep. Ten milligrams is frequently enough; others need 10 to 80 milligrams.

Light suppresses melatonin production in human beings, and therefore melatonin production seems to go up in the winter leading to some people having depression. On the other hand, if you take the melatonin earlier and get people sleeping better, sometimes you can avoid the winter depression. Early morning light, 2500 to 10,000 lux maybe is another way to get people out of the winter blues, gently nudging the sleep cycle. During this winter depression cycle, patients may appear to be bipolar type II, have temporal lobe disorder or atypical depression. This of course, represents brain chemical imbalance which also occurs in the aged with low urinary melatonin metabolite secretion.

High Blood Pressure/ Wound Healing

High blood pressure wound healing has gone awry, according to a new study. Wound healing is actually a metaphor applying to the biochemistry of the heart when an excess number of chemicals, such as angiotensin and aldosterone exceed the good chemicals and natural steroids in the body. Essentially, aging is a loss of DHEA, testosterone and estrogens which allow the heart to become damaged. Fibrous tissue appears in the heart and the heart becomes wounded.

Steroids, fish oils and natural hormones can repair these wounds.

According to a recent Sept. 21, 1994 *Journal of the American Medical Association,* report, lifestyle changes and low dose diuretics should be the first choice in treatment of hypertension in the elderly.

Addiction

OVERCOMING CIGARETTE AND FOOD ADDICTION THAT RAISES BLOOD PRESSURE

Learning to break addictive patterns is the most critical dimension of nutrition and preventive medicine. Addictive patterns of behavior always lead to poor nutrition and diseases that could have been prevented. How is this so? It is because of our new understanding of what addiction is. Addiction is not just limited to dangerous drugs such as heroin, LSD, crack, cocaine and amphetamines, but addiction is also found to occur in less serious substances such as alcohol, cigarettes and caffeine, and even less serious substances than these, such as carbohydrates, sugar, fat, junk food and even with people in codependent and addictive relationships. Addiction by our definition is any behavior that a person does repetitively that they know is dangerous for them or destructive or unhealthy but for a variety of reasons are unable, by will power, to stop that behavior.

When we understand addiction as repetitive, compulsive, destructive behavior that a person cannot stop through will power, addiction then becomes the root of most of our chronic diseases. We all know now that the search for higher consciousness in the '60s led to lower consciousness and brain injury. The strong drugs, from LSD to heroin, all cause brain damage, as does alcohol, and even cigarette smoking puts an individual at the highest risk for developing Alzheimer's disease, due to microvascular blockage and cerebral vascular dementias. We also know that caffeine causes pancreatic cancer and alcohol may be linked to breast cancer and many other chronic diseases. It is eating addiction that indirectly produces obesity, diabetes, hypertension. Therefore virtually all the major killers in our society are linked to repetitive, destructive, addictive behavior. Obesity and a high fat diet, leads to cancer and more heart diseases. There is nothing more critical in our society for nutrition and preventive medicine than to be able to teach and do the techniques that will break the addictive cycle.

In the field of preventive medicine, all of us are trying to get our patients to increase their fiber intake, stop smoking, give up caffeine and alcohol, remove refined sugars and carbohydrates, exercise regularly, to have positive and productive relationships with their loved ones, to get appropriate amounts of rest, to avoid fried foods and salty foods, excessive spicy foods, smoked meat and to transform their healthy emotional lifestyle into a diet of lean protein, high fiber, low fat, regular, balanced and other appropriate health goals.

It appears that most patients fall off the band wagon of diet relatively quickly and the pattern of lifestyle often returns to its previous functioning. Attempts to restructure a person's health away from addiction is difficult. Therapy has been tried, antidepressants have been tried. Medications to motivate the individual from pondimin to tenuate, from Prozac to Welbutrin can be used to certain degrees, but most patients still tend to return to bad habits, particularly their addictive bad habits with food, drugs, relationships; anything from ice cream to LSD.

What is the source of this repetitive destructive behavior? Sigmund Freud called it the death instinct, the compulsion to repeat. Others call it the quest and desire for ritual. What is it in the body that causes this cycling?

Historically we have learned from plagues. Scurvy taught us the value of vitamin C, beri-beri taught us the value of B1 and pellagra taught us the miracle of niacin. The plague of drug abuse has taught us something about repetitive, destructive behavior that affects every individual. Although fewer people are becoming addicted to the dangerous drugs, a great majority, if not all Americans have repetitive, destructive behaviors that they can not break. The technique of cranial electrical stimulation (CES) has been so helpful in helping drug abusers withdraw from drugs and break their addictive patterns and has even greater consequences for the average neurotic and health-oriented patient. The average severe drug abuser frequently needs medication along with CES because of the advanced brain disease that has occurred either as a result of preexisting brain disease or as a result of drug abuse. The wider applications of CES are on a day-to-day preventive nature of preventing drug abuse in adolescents and deterioration into bad habits of white flour, junk food, sugar, coffee and cigarette addiction for a large group of Americans.

Any health practitioner who has ever dealt with a patient who cannot execute his/her good advice for the patient must now recognize that patients have addictive behavioral patterns which can be dealt with on a psychotherapeutic, spiritual, emotional level.

The *Journal of the American Medical Association* reported that recent studies indicated that your blood pressure affects your whole brain function, which will result in significant impairment of cognitive function. The cognitive impairment found in hypertensive patients includes acquired deficit memory function, problem solving, orientation and abstraction, and diminishes an individual's capacity to function independently, and is a major component of dementing diseases. These were determined in a variety of dementia scales, minimental state exams and neurocognitive analysis.

Save your brain . . . lower your blood pressure!

Appendix

Dr. Braverman's Special Formulas (Typical Examples)

Product Hypertension Formula (#1)

Niacinamide	75 mg
Ascorbic acid	60 mg
Pyridoxine HCL	75 mg
Garlic powder	300 mg
Taurine	300 mg
Magnesium oxide	(mg 60%) 125 mg
Potassium chloride	(K 50%) 20 mg
Beta-carotene	(10%) 12 mg
Zinc chelate	(Zn 12.5%) 50 mg
Molybdenum chelate	(Mo 0.2%) 30 mg
Chromium chloride	(Cr 20%) 0.2 mg
Sodium selenite	(Se 45%) 0.07 mg

Product Antioxidant Formula (#2)

Ascorbic acid	250 mg
Niacinamide	12.5 mg
L-Cysteine	500 mg
Beta-carotene	10% 12,500 IU (75 mg)
Vitamin E	200 IU (400 mg)

Sodium selenite   (45% Se) 220 mcg

Product Calcium Formula (#3)

Oyster shell   (30% CA) 1335 mg
Manganese chelate   (10%) 200 mg
Vitamin D3   100,000 IU per gram,
                                2 mg

Note: We are changing to calcium citrate and adding .5 mg
Boron for better absorption.

Product Magnesium Formula (#4)

Vitamin B6   100 mg
Magnesium oxide   (Mg 60%) 1167 mg
Zinc chelate   (Zn 12.5%) 160 mg

Product Tryptophan Formula (#5)

L-Tryptophan   450 mg
Niacinamide   225 mg
Niacin   25 mg
Choline bitartrate   80 mg

Product Multi Formula (#9)

Ascorbic acid   300 mg
Niacinamide   15 mg
B2   8 mg
B6   8 mg
Niacin   10 mg

B1 80%	10 mg
B12 1%	3 mg
d-Cal pantothenate	11 mg
Biotin 1%	7.5 mg
Vitamin C	300 mg
Vitamin D	400 IU
Vitamin E	60 mg
Vitamin A	4000 IU
Oyster shell	400 mg
Magnesium oxide	50 mg
Molybdenum chelate .2%	12.5 mg
Manganese chelate 20%	1 mg
Zinc (chelate) 12.5%	8 mg
Iron (chelate) 10%	8 mg
Iodine (kelp) 5%	150 mcg
Copper (chelate) 10%	.5 mg
Chromium GTF	100 mcg
Calcium (carbonate)	120 mg

Product Amino-Stim Formula (#10)

DL-Phenylalanine	350 mg
L-Tyrosine	200 mg
Methionine	100 mg
Octacosanol (5%)	60 mg

Bibliography

Mannion, J. D., M.D., et al., Acute Electrical Stimulation Increases Extramyocardial Collateral Blood Flow After a Cardiomyoplasty, *Ann Thoriac Surg* 1993;56:1351-8.

Markovitz, J. H., M.D., et al., Psychological Predictors of Hypertension in the Framingham Study, *JAMA,* Nov. 24, 1993, vol. 270, no. 20.

Pickering, T. G., M.D., DPhil, Tension and Hypertension, *JAMA,* Nov. 24, 1993, vol. 270, no. 20.

Sharma, A. M., et al., Effect of Dietary Salt Restriction on Urinary Serotonin and 5-Hydroxyindoleacetic Acid Execretion in Man, *Journal of Hypertension* 1993; 11:1381-1386.

Undo Pressure: Taking Control May Help Fight Hypertension, *Prevention,* Jan. 1994, pp. 17-18.

Index

addiction, 162, 191–193
aerobic exercise, 178
aggression, 156–157
aging, 190–191
alcohol, 27, 75, 192
allergies, and biofeedback, 174
alpha waves, 165, 170
alpha-blockers, 5–6, 9, 68
Alzheimer's disease, 192
amino acids, 140, 146, 161
  in hypertension therapy, 21
  and salt appetite, 107
  see also homocysteine; melatonin;
    methionine; tryptophan
andropause, 184–186
anger, 156–157
angiotensin, 7, 68–69
animal foods, 25
Antakarana, 165
anticoagulants, 150–151
antidepressants, 161
antioxidants, 181
anxiety see stress
appetite suppressants, 71
arrhythmias, 79, 135
atherosclerosis, 66, 121, 155

BEAM machine, 158–159
beta-blockers, 3, 5–6, 68
  case histories, 87–88
beverages, 26
  recipes, 39, 41–44, 54
biochemical individuality, 85
biofeedback, 153, 163–174
blood clots, 112–113
blood pressure, 105–106, 113
  and biofeedback, 170–171
  and brain function, 193
  measuring, 109–110, 117–118

blood pressure (*continued*)
  monitoring, 134–135
  see also hypertension
blood tests, 120
body composition analysis, 84, 130–134
body fat, 131–132
borage oil, 84
brain bioelectrical approach see cranial
  electrotherapy stimulations
brain wave training see biofeedback
Braverman Plan see nutritional
  therapy
butter (recipe), 40
bypass surgery, and magnesium, 152

cadmium, 82, 83
caffeine, 75, 192
calcification, 176
calcium, 20, 75, 78–79, 81, 113
  deficiency, 141
  and EDTA, 174
  supplements, 60
calcium channel blockers, 8, 16, 69,
  176
calcium citrate, 78
calories, restaurant substitutions, 57
cancer
  and diet, 146
  and hypertension, 65
  and visualization, 165
capsicum peppers, 112–113
Captopril, 69
cardiac reversal, 155
cardiomyopathy, and vitamin E, 181
cardiovascular disease
  deaths, 65
  risk factors, 125
  symptoms, 126
  and vegetarian diets, 144

201

estriol, 188
estrogen, 187–188
ethylene diamine tetraacetic acid, 18, 174
exercise, 13, 61, 71, 72, 112, 176–179

familial hypercholesteremia, 71
fats and oils, 27–28, 75–76, 114
  in hypertension therapy, 19
  low fat substitutes, 136–137
  and serum cholesterol, 73
  sources, 112
  see also fatty acids; fish oil; polyunsaturated oils
fatty acids, 29
fertility, 183
FES see fine electrical stimulator
fiber, 22, 73
fillet souffle (recipe), 47
fine electrical stimulator, 158, 159–160
fish, recipes, 45–47
fish oil, 76, 113, 154
  and HDL cholesterol, 180
folic acid, 154
food diary, 24
foods
  disease fighting, 147–150
  fresh, 73
  and hypertension, 29–30
fruit, 26

galanin, 107
garlic, 22, 84, 113
gastric cancer, and sodium, 81
genetics, and hypertension, 85
glucose intolerance, 68, 72, 74, 137–138
glutamine, 138
grains, 25, 142

health salad (recipe), 53
healthy heart spread (recipe), 52
heart attacks, and beta-blockers, 68
heart disease, reversal of, 154
Heart Formula, 94–95
heart rhythms, 115, 135
heavy metals
  and cholesterol, 18
  and vitamin C, 180
  and zinc, 180
high blood pressure see hypertension
high blood pressure wound healing, 190–191
high carbohydrate diet, and glucose intolerance, 74

Holter monitors, 135
homocysteine, 154
hydralazine, 9
hypercalcemia, 80
hypercholesterolemia, 71
hypertension, 1–2
  case histories, 86–93, 97–104
  causes of, 84, 110
  and diet, 29–30, 70
  see also diet therapy; nutritional therapy
  drug therapy see hypertension drugs
  epidemiology, 65–66
  mild symptoms, 106
  and nutrition, 64
  see also diet therapy; nutritional therapy
  prognosis factors, 106
  psychological factors, 111, 153–154
  reversal of, 154
  risk factors, 108
hypertension drugs, 2–10, 66–67, 110–111
  and aged, 66
  case history, 86–87
  costs, 10–11
  daily regimen, 12–15
  reduction in use, 61, 93–94
  risk factors, 3–10, 67–70
  and sex drive, 108
  see also alpha-blockers; angiotensin; beta-blockers; diuretics; methyldopa; vasodilators
hypertension shakes, recipes, 41–44
hypoglycemia, 24, 151

immune system, and stress, 168
impedance plethysmography, 133
impotence, 183–184, 186
infertility, 183
insomnia, and CES, 158

Jacob's ladder, 165
jicama-chili pepper relish (recipe), 48
Jiva, 172

labile high blood pressure, 110
lactovegetarians, 72, 141
lead, 83
leafy vegetables, 26
left ventricular hypertrophy, 134
leg cramps, 179
lemonade (recipe), 54

About the Author

Eric R. Braverman, M.D. is currently director of the Princeton Associates for Total Health (PATH) Center in Princeton, New Jersey. He is the former director of research at the Robert C. Atkins Center for Alternative Therapies in New York City, and former chief clinical researcher at the Princeton Brain Bio Center.

Dr. Braverman hosted the popular syndicated New York City ABC radio show "Total Health," which he now presents on WMCA in New York City and also on WTTM in Trenton and Philadelphia.

Dr. Braverman's health advice column appears bimonthly in *Total Health* magazine. His medical advice has also appeared in numerous mass market magazines, including *Harper's Bazaar* and *Let's Live*. He has contributed over 100 medical articles to scientific periodicals and journals. In April 1987, Keats published his first book, *The Healing Nutrients Within: Facts, Findings and the New Research on Amino Acids,* now in a second printing. This pioneering work relates to the use of amino acids in reversing aging, building muscle, curing insomnia, treating hyperactivity, depression, schizophrenia, heart failure, hypertension, cholesterol conditions, toxic chemical syndromes and cancer. His new *PATH Wellness Manual* (1994) continues this great tradition.

Dr. Braverman attended Brandeis University where he graduated summa cum laude, Phi Beta Kappa, with a B.A. degree. While at Brandeis, Dr. Braverman conducted re-

About the Author

search in the Genetics Unit at the Harvard Medical School at Massachusetts General Hospital.

After graduation, he attended New York University Medical School where he received his M.D. degree with honors in 1983.

At N.Y.U., he conducted research on the isolated living brain, and after training in internal medicine at a Yale Medical School affiliate hospital, he received the Physicians Recognition Award from the American Medical Association. He has lectured at the TMJ Pain Program of the New Jersey Medical School in Newark, and has been an elective instructor in nutrition at the Columbia School of Physicians and Surgeons as well.

Dr. Braverman is on the editorial boards of the *Journal of Applied Nutrition* and the *Journal of Brain Dysfunction.* He collaborates closely with Kenneth Blum, Ph.D., Professor of Pharmacology at the University of Texas, on research in such diverse fields as genetics, addiction, obesity, psychiatry, and heart disease.